Leonidas Spratt

Man in Continuation at this Earth of a Nature of Reality throughout the Universe

By Tradition of that Reality from its original Universe of Force

Leonidas Spratt

Man in Continuation at this Earth of a Nature of Reality throughout the Universe
By Tradition of that Reality from its original Universe of Force

ISBN/EAN: 9783337216450

Printed in Europe, USA, Canada, Australia, Japan

Cover: Foto ©ninafisch / pixelio.de

More available books at **www.hansebooks.com**

MAN

IN CONTINUATION AT THIS EARTH

OF

A Nature of Reality Throughout the Universe

BY

TRADITION OF THAT REALITY FROM ITS ORIGINAL UNIVERSE OF FORCE.

BY

LEONIDAS SPRATT.

WASHINGTON, D. C.:
GIBSON BROS., PRINTERS AND BOOKBINDERS.
1894.

The following papers were prepared as preface and introduction to an argument upon the subject of "Man in Continuation of Nature," but they have become voluminous; and, as they contain an outline of the argument, I have thought it best to publish them to themselves, that the argument, itself heavy enough, will be relieved of that unnecessary weight.

LEONIDAS SPRATT.

MAN IN CONTINUATION OF NATURE.

PREFACE.

To MAN the truth of his relation to nature is important. There is a course of being we term nature through stars, sun, earth, plant, and animal from the universe to man: and to him it is important to know whether he, also, be of this nature or not. If he be, he is of it but as are other natures; and to be but his most and best at his time and place possible; and, to test the question whether he be of nature or not, I have proposed that he be in continuation of nature. He can be in continuation of nature but as he be of nature. But he can be of nature but as he be in the course of the resolutions of that being from the universe of which is nature. Of this he can be but as at his time and place he be his best and most; and this simply: and as a crucial test, not only of the truth that man is of nature but that he is in nature but to be his most and best, it is proposed that he is in continuation of nature. And to this it is contended that there is reality. That there is infinite being finite; and this the word of God; and this an universe of force of which at this earth there are the physical forces, heat, light, electricity and magnetism—dynamic in that seeming vacuum we term space and static in that apparent plenum we term matter—and that of this there is nature. And it is intended that of this there is nature; and, first, for the reason that there is a nature for which there were no other source; and next for that the reality is being physiological, and capable, as such, of teleologic evo-involution into the beings possible from the universe to man. That man in organic matter at this earth is such being physiological in teleologic evo-involution into the man possible. That in this he is in continuation at this earth of a nature of reality throughout the universe. And that this—the theory of man in continuation of nature—is dependent for its truth but upon the condition that there be such original reality in an universe of force. And that while there is no such reality visible to man there is the hypothesis of such reality as the condition of every phenomenon to man, no one of which were possible, or other than the miracle of consequence without cause, if there be not cause in such reality. And that there are the natures from the universe to man inclusive by deduction from such hypothesis, which itself were the miracle of cause without consequence if there be not such natures as truly as that every nature were the miracle of consequence without cause if there be not cause in such hypothesis. And that there is man of such nature as well for the reason that he were else the miracle of consequence without cause as for that he is in fact such being physiological in teleologic evoinvolution not only into the unilateral man of a single race of man existing now, but into a better and more abundant man of unequal races in relations of inequality.

It is contended that the present man is not the man possible—that he is not the most possible or the best possible that he be his most. That there are vast tracts of this earth's surface unoccupied by man; that of that occupied there is scarce an acre so cultivated as to produce its most in support of man; and that there is room enough upon this earth under proper cultivation for a million to the one of man upon it now. That even monogamic man, now the best, from the infirmities of his social constitution cannot advance to such occupation of the earth; that no monogamic state can long survive the dominion of its proletariate. That this is the power to administer a state in these who do not furnish a means to its support. That this is a lethal agent of decadence and dissolution. And that of this in every monogamic state there is scarcely the period of maturity before the process of decadence begins, to end in dissolution—with no state surviving. After which the state to populate the place must start *de novo*. That every such state is without the conditions of a constitution; that these can possibly exist but in a state of unequal races in relations of inequality; and that of such states, only, is there to be the ultimate population of this earth.

There are now unequal orders of the human race. The agamic man is unequal to the polygamic, and the polygamic to the monogamic man, in their respective abilities to procure the means of subsistence and support. But the greater the respective differentiations from the neutral human being intermediate the greater is their fitness for concurrence in such man. As upon the ineradicable differences of parents male and female depends their ability to unite in production of a family, so different are the agamic savages of Africa and the monogamic citizens of Europe. And it is intended that of an union of these races there were bilateral states as much above the simple agamic or monogamic state as is the family agamic, polygamic, or monogamic to the parents who produce it.

Such was the man of agamic blacks and monogamic whites lately in union in these Southern states. And it is contended that such union of such races is necessary to the man possible and that in this Southern man there was the potency and promise of the largest, best and most abundant man this world has known. And that this is not an inconsiderate conception, or an expression of impatience merely at the results of our experiences, or even an afterthought from consequences however these be fitted to suggest it, but is a matured opinion from anxious consideration of the subject, my utterances and activities in that period before the war when issues were made up, will show.

PREFACE.

In 1853 I had charge of the "Standard," a paper at Charleston, S. C.—of no great importance—and fated to an early end, and, possibly, through my mismanagement,—though, started to an occasion, it is doubtful if it could have long survived it. Some years before, the state had nullified an act of congress and from compromises offered had receded from her ordinance. But the compromises were not kept. It was complained by the people of that state that the tariff acts of congress in protection of industries at the North were of injury to the South. And in response to the ordinance by another act of congress the evil was abated somewhat, but by later acts the duties were not only reimposed but increased. With this the spirit of resistance was again aroused, and,—the sufficiency of nullification having become questioned,—the measure of secession was proposed; and, with respect to this, the only question was,—or seemed to be,—whether this state should await the "co-operation" of other Southern states or go alone; and to resist the separate action of the state the Standard was established; and the resistance was successful.

The sense of the state expressed in 1852 was against the measure of separate state action, and,—the Standard of victory then without further office,—I was at liberty to adopt what policy I pleased. And I was pleased with that of a revival of the foreign slave-trade,—at least to the extent of removing from it the censures and restrictions of the general government. The foreign slave-trade had brought the slaves there were to the South, but had been suppressed as piracy by act of congress in 1808, at which time the states admitting slavery were the more potent and progressive; but from that time forward the slave states advanced but by natural increase; and the "free" states as they were called, by this and by an average of near 250,000 pauper laborers yearly from abroad. In each there was its special civilization, and that of the North had thus become the stronger. And more than that, it had become distinctively proletariate in the recognition of the right of those to rule the state not participating in the proprietary contributions to sustain the state.

There is man, as I have said, but in the family agamic, polygamic, and monogamic. And agamic in the children, infant and adult, about a store of provisions in the hands of their unmarried mother. And polygamic in such children of several mothers about a store in the hands of their single father. And monogamic in such children of a single mother about a store in the hands of a single father. And the agamic man in savage stocks; and the polygamic in barbarous tribes; and the monogamic in civil states; with a possible man in an union of monogamic and agamic families, the one white and the other black, about a store in the hands of the white male parent and master to sustain them both in one.

And as in theory of the monogamic state,—the

only one to be considered,—there is this but of monogamic families,—and these in subsistence and safety but upon a store of provisions in the hands of the male parent,—the state itself can be in subsistence and safety but upon a store contributed by proprietary male parents, who only therefore can rightfully have suffrage with respect to it. And in result of such proprietary parental suffrage in application of such store to the uses of the state there is its government to be termed *patriate*. But from indolence, inefficiency, calamity, or crime, parents cease to be proprietary without forfeiture of franchise; and adult males, not parents, acquire the right to vote; and—if this be not enough to the dissolution of the state—adult females must acquire that right; and if this be not enough, infants, male and female, must acquire that right; so that in time there comes to be a very large majority of these not contributing to the support of the state who have power to dispose—and to their own uses—of the fund upon which the state subsists: That majority in every monogamic state becomes the state. There is no restriction of its volition in a constitution it interprets. It is an intrusive and abnormal being, therefore, and not in support but in subversion of the state, which therefore becomes the car for all to ride on but none to pull; and its government a game of pool, at which the players order the propertied party to put up the stakes they play for.

The state under the proprietary parents who support the state is a state of offspring controlled by parents and termed *patriate*. The state under those who do not support it is one of parents controlled by offspring. And the one the *patriate*, the other is the *proletariate* state; and as the proclivities of individual interests are resistless; as every being in nature is charged with the continuation of its own existence without the power to exist for any other; and as to this rule the man is no exception, as he cannot of thought add a cubit to his stature, or at his time and place be other than he is or originate a motive to his own volition—this proletariate must loot the patriate state. The wage-earner will have more pay for less work. Industries combining will be protected at the expense of others; pensions will be allowed and drawn under evĕry possible pretext of service; salaried men and millionaires will make visible investments but in property abroad, or in the bonds of the government not taxed; and men and women will quit the continuation of their race on marriage for sensual indulgences without it. Such and so proletariate in principle were the states of the North at the time referred to. And that proletariate practically supreme in every Northern state was also in virtue of their larger population soon to be supreme in congress, and taking what it wanted through the legislatures of the Northern states it was about to take through congress what it wanted of the South. Against this there was no appeal even to its lucid moments, which could not possibly occur. And it was as remorseless as fate for the reason simply that it was as blind. Of this was the House of Commons in 1832, which could see in the reform bill but that upon this depended the re-election of its members. And of this the Lords, who could see but that upon this depended their exemption from a deluge of new-created peers. And of this the judges of the supreme court of the United States, who, after a week of oratory, could see but as they saw at first, that Mr. Hayes was of the proletariate faction represented by the one part of that body and Mr. Tilden of that represented by the other, and that there was nothing to be done but to let the decision rest upon their respective numbers. And such the proletariate,—an inverted nature to extinguish human life and a lethal reptile to form and crawl and feed upon the vitals of the state as larval insects feed upon the carcass of their host,—against this there was resistance but in counter action; and this but in the introduction of another race sufficient for the offices of labor under a higher race but without participation in its direction. Such I assumed to be the negro under the whites in the Southern states; and,—with such a population of a weaker in subordination to a stronger race of man,—that no proletariate in any monogamic state could form.

I was assured that with that trade reopened there would have been slaves at importers' prices and that at these every capable white man could and would have owned his slave. That so he had been a slavery propagandist,—that there would have been owners not only at the South but to the North of the line between the States; and that with greater integrity than had been greater territory to the South. Nor was it necessary that the trade should have been reopened by the South: legitimated, northern capital had imported slaves to the utmost requisition North or South. And so in considering the fortunes of the South it seemed to her material interests at least that the trade should be legitimated. And it was becoming, also, that it should be. If the trade were piracy the slave was plunder, and it was not only unbecoming but immoral to hold property the procurement of which was justly branded as a crime, and our acquiescence in the action of the government imposing such brand was an admission of its justice.

Nor did it seem that even the proletariate North would seriously oppose the removal of the brand. It wanted and was bound to have what it could take by proletariate legislation from the South; and the richer and fatter that might be the better. And the South had been richer and the Union richer from the importation of foreign slaves. They would have supplied the want of slaves at the South quite inadequate to her possible industries and to the requisitions of a growing West, and they would have come in the place of pauper laborers from abroad and had been more productive and not in competition with wage-earners at the North but to their support, the every one of whom could and would have owned his slave at importers' prices ; and they could and would have taken bleeding Kansas and extended slavery from Missouri to the Pacific, and probably northward to the line of Canada.

It is possible that upon this extended state the proletariate then existing in the republican party would have lost its grip. But of this danger it would have been unconscious. And I am quite assured that if the South had presented to the North the alternative of the slave-trade or secession, the North would have readily accepted the slave-trade and that our differences had been composed. The North would have persisted in a sectional presidency, but the significance of that movement would have been different. The South, satisfied with the ultimate security of her civilization, would have been indifferent to such movement, and even have given her vote as she had often done to a Northern man; and instead of a proletariate without a constitution other than that the proletariate may interpret to its uses, there had been a state with a constitution the best possible and the only constitution to a monogamic people possible, and this in the ineradicable differences of unequal races united in relations of inequality.

But the merit of this policy was in its adoption, only, at that time : and convinced then of its importance as I am now, and that the peace, safety, fortunes, and the fate of this republic depended on it, with a wearying pertinacity I did to its adoption what I could. I put it before the South by articles in my own paper and before the South and North by articles so written as to force their entrance to the Herald, Times and Tribune, and to its popular consideration I kept it for years before the commercial convention of the Southern states. There had been an annual convention of Southern gentlemen to questions of Southern policy before whom at Savannah in 1856 I placed the resolution that as a measure of Southern policy the trade be reopened. This was debated for the week to the exclusion of other subjects, and again at Knoxville in 1857, and at Montgomery in 1858, and at Vicksburg in 1859, where it was finally adopted and referred as an expression of Southern sentiment to Southern people.

But before there was more decisive action Mr. Lincoln was elected as a sectional president; and there was secession; and the holding of Fort Sumter; and the firing on it consequent; and invasion, and the war, and subjugation of the South and the liberation of her slaves; and this to the general satisfaction, it would seem, of this country and the world.

The proletariate North is satisfied as nearly as that monster may be in the millions of money it may take to protected industries and pensions. And the South, now as proletariate as the North, is satisfied—as many of her distinguished men declare—at least in her freedom from an odious institution and her admission to the swim of a proletariate democracy. And the world generally is satisfied with the establishment here of a proletariate state,—for the reason expressed that it is matter they had nothing to do with,—but for the real reason that all monogamic states are becoming as proletariate as this; and that in all the monogamic world, at least, there has been satisfaction at the subjugation of the South in her effort to sustain a counteraction to such proletariate. But believing that that tendency prevails in every monogamic state; and that it is death to the state as the patriate is life; and that the South was in travail, not for herself but humanity, in sustaining the relation of inequality among unequals,—the one sole condition upon which man can rise to a civilization better than that consisting in the existence of the state under the inflictions of a popular or other irresponsible power sensible of its immediate wants but unconscious of its ulterior interests in the preservation of the state—however unimportant or uninteresting the fact may be, I did not then and do not now concur in that accord and satisfaction so generally expressed.

I did not and do not see that the white race at the South could or can sustain itself to its earlier moral elevation without the physical supports of a weaker race; or that the negro here could or can sustain himself to continued existence in competition with the whites; or that he could be deported, or that he could perpetuate his black race by its miscegenation with the white; or that while the one race was lowered the other was not to be exterminated. Nor did I see but that the Northern states themselves, discharged of the supports of such Southern civilization, were more irrevocably turned to the proletariate, which would not spare them if it could and could not if it would, more than the larval insects could spare the carcass of their host, or than the Roman proletariate the state of Rome. The Roman proletariate in possession of the Roman state through the consul appointed by its preoccupation of the forum on the day of the election demanded of the consul so appointed corn and wine and oil from Asia and Africa, and shows and gladiatorial exhibitions to amuse it on its delirious way to its own destruction and the dissolution of the state.

And this proletariate, possessed of the legislatures of the states, and congress through preoccupation of precincts on the days of election, must demand indulgences equally fatal to the state as to themselves. I doubt if there be a legislator, judge or governor in all these states in office for reasons of his admitted virtues, but in spite of them; or that there is one who will continue in office after it is found he will not do the work for which he was elected. And for these reasons and apart from my personal experiences and disappointments in the matter I am not satisfied that the North has so suppressed the civilization of the South. But believing that it was a calamity to the South and an injury to the North, and a wrong to that man in nature of this universe whom God intended and whom God intends, and that it rolled back that tide of time which was bearing unnumbered blessings to the present man, I submit this argument *de bene esse* and for what it may be worth to the truth of that belief.

It will not be popular. It proposes an impersonal God and that man to his being possible must submit to inequalities in that being possible; and to neither of these propositions is proletariate man inclined, and to him the proposition is addressed.

There is no state of Europe or America not monogamic of a single race; and no such state not proletariate in its administration by these not contributing the fund upon which the state subsists. In the constitutional kingdoms of Europe there are the traditions of their polygamic states. Their kings and lords, however they may be named, are the consequences without cause, if they be not consequences by tradition from antecedent tribal states existing but of polygamic man. These are not in representation of the funds they contribute to the state but of a power to dispose them to their uses; nor the more is the Commons, supreme in England, or the legislature of the states and the congress of this Union— no member of whom is in his place but by suffrage of those not contributing the fund administered. And the forum I address is as proletariate, therefore, as was that of Rome, in which by preoccupying the forum it determined the consul through whom it was allowed the plunder of that state.

And this man will not accept an impersonal God. Such God can only hold his universe of life and nature to the resolutions of its life into the natures of it possible and into man at this earth as to natures intermediate, in consistence with which the man only can live, who, complying with the conditions at his time and place, should live. But to the individual man this justice is not what he wants, but favor; and all are induced by their solicitudes to feel that there is a precable anthropomorphic being in moral likeness of themselves who by proper incantations can be made to turn the scales of justice to mercy for them, however it be in wrath to others. And they cannot favor the truth, whatever the reason for it, that defeats them of such God. Nor the more readily can they accept the equally offensive truth that they are to take but that position they can get by merit in the states of man. He insists that he may supplement his merit by address. He has no repugnance to inequalities of position provided some other be subordinate to him, but he has great repugnance to the truth that he may be subordinate to some one else. In analysis of the proletariate there is agrarianism; and of agrarianism anarchy; and of anarchy,—not that there be not upper and lower classes, but that there be not a class above the one in which is the anarchist himself, who were miserable there if there be not some below him. And the man of this age generally cannot accept of either proposition but in sacrifice of feelings he will not make.

But whatever be his feeling he must accept it if it be true. And it is true not only that there is an impersonal God and man in inequalities but that there is such man in continuation of the nature of the universe if there be nature ; and that there is nature if there be God, or being finite, or force, or space, or matter, or life, or nature, or the universe, or star, or sun, or earth, or plant, or animal, or man, or conscience in man, or ideality in conscience,—not one of which were possible, or other than the miracle of cause without consequence or consequence without cause if there be not such nature of which man is so in continuation at this earth.

Since the fall of slavery here such man of unequal races may not recur at once, but man is destined to an extended period of existence at this earth. States will fall as will individuals, but the race will roll on and with accumulating volume while there are yet at this earth the conditions of human existence, and the truth can wait; as that of this earth upon the sun ; and of the plant upon the earth ; and of the animal upon the plant ; and of man upon the animal ; and of polygamic upon agamic man ; and of monogamic upon polygamic man. And that when the history of these states shall have been lost in a fabulous antiquity, if not sooner, there will be,—and upon this soil,—a people of human races so related : and this as abundant in blessings and as prodigal in promise as were lately the people of these Southern states, themselves at their time the most abundant of blessings and prodigal of promise the sun has ever shone on.

Such is the proposition of man at this earth in continuation of a nature of reality throughout the universe by tradition of an original reality in force of the finite word of God. It intends that of the reality in resolution there is nature; and from the universe to man; and that man is of nature; and in continuation of nature to the man possible; and him the most and best man possible that he be his most. And it is intended that the truth of this proposition is contingent but upon the truth of that hypothesis.

Intending that there is reality of the word of God in an universe of force, it intends that this is being physiological; and this the being possible of kindred beings different of their reciprocal affinities simply in reciprocal limitations of each other, in wheels of being static in revolutions on axes of beings dynamic; that these are in teleologic evo-involution; and that of the physiological universe of these in such resolution there are stars about the axes of the universe, and suns about the stars, and the earth about the sun, and the plant about the earth, and the animal about the plant, and the man about the animal, of whom in such process continued, there is agamic man of the animal, and polygamic of agamic man, and monogamic of polygamic man, and that there is, or is to be, compound man in an union of unequal races of the pre-existing race; and that in these there is nature, and that these are natures, and that each is but the nature possible of life into it from the universe in resolution.

It intends that each nature is static being and in life of motive from the dynamic axis of the universe, and that of such motive it is the nature possible.

And intended that motive is cause and nature consequence, it is intended that each such successive nature possible is the consequence possible of cause possible in such motive to produce it; and that in this there is to each nature but the cause possible; and in each nature but the consequence possible of that creative cause; and that other, or more, or less than the cause possible to the nature possible of that cause were the miracle of cause without consequence; and that other, or more, or less than the nature possible of that cause possible were the miracle of consequence without cause.

And intended that motive is life and life cause, it is intended, and for the same reason, that there is life but to nature possible, and nature but of life possible, and that every nature therefore is simply to its most possible, and, to its best possible, that it be its most of the life possible in tradition from the universe of force; and that such simply is man; that he is but the nature possible but of his life possible as cause through nature; and that this cause in man were the miracle of cause without consequence if there be not ultimately in nature the man possible; and if in being so he be not his most possible and his best possible that he be his most. And such the proposition of man in continuation of nature it is presented as a crucial test of man's relation to nature which I have said it is important he should know, and also to emphasize the truth that he is in nature; and in nature but to his ends in nature; and to his ends in nature but in consistence with the conditions of his being thus the most abundant man possible; and the best man possible that he be the most abundant; and it had been policy, perhaps, to have presented this theory in parts.

There are men of science and philosophy who are forced to accept nature from an universe of life in force, and man from nature, but who are not so forced to project man to the man possible; and there are men not of speculation but of work in being possible to whom it is important to know what the possible of man is, that they may work up to it. To the one of these the theory of nature, only, of man in nature were apt to be interesting; to the others the means and ends of man in nature, only, were apt to be so, and the science of the past were as inapt to accept the business of the future as the business of the future to accept the science of the past. And if I were concerned about the profits or the popularity of my work it had been policy, doubtless, to have given it in parts, and to men in science and in business the subjects they would consider without the others that they would not. But without pretending to excessive magnanimity, I am more concerned about the future fortunes of the race of man than the popularity or profits of this effort to address him, and assured that man will ultimately attain to his possible fortunes, and this through the union of unequal races I suggest, I am yet assured he will the more readily do so under the proclivities of a preconception of that state.

If when I first proposed the foreign slave-trade to the further progress of man in this state of states united,—and of man in other states under the tractile force of its example,—I could have fixed in the minds of its people a sense of the truth that in such union of unequal races as there was in the Southern states there was the way to a higher and better state of man than had been, the North had not so warred upon the South, the South had not been forced to so resist the North; a *modus vivendi* had been established; and not only would the calamities of the war have been averted but incalculable ages had been added to the life in nature of this republic. Grand as it now is in the plenitude of its unorganized life into nature possible, it is unreasonable that its nature now provisionally possible can long survive the ferments of dissolution now at work upon it. Unilateral of but a single race, with no constitution other than that consisting in the resolutions of such single race,— as potent to control its action as are the resolutions of the individual he at any time may reconsider,—it is unreasonable that under such paper constitution simply it can resist to its ends,—otherwise possible,—

the party in power that would use it to *its* ends; but under a constitution of ineradicably different races combined to the ends of a common subsistence and safety among other peoples not so situated, and to whom such constitution, therefore, is now and for the time at least impossible, there is no reason why the states of the South should not have been as enduring as her hills, or why the states of the North, associated with such stable Southern states, had not been as enduring as these states of the South themselves. This opportunity was lost; but in the countless ages of man's existence yet upon this earth it may and must occur again. The proclivities of a preconception of this truth must act then as it would have lately here, and it is important that it be fixed upon the mind of man. It can be so fixed by its association with the truth of a nature of reality in which is man, who cannot otherwise than attain to his ends but in relations of inequality. And concerned but in the fortunes of man, with the assurance that nature—as she has done—can take care of herself, I forego what of advantage there might have been in serving my entertainment in parts to the tastes of those inclined to partake of it, and will allow no one to accept the promises of a nature in the resolutions of an universe of force who does not also accept man in his way to the man possible through an ultimate union of unequal races to that end.

And such the proposition that there is a man in

continuation of nature so tediously stated, it may seem that the argument to support it might now begin; but its truth is for man's consideration. He it is who at the present time must accept it or reject it. Every nature from the universe to man accepts its nature thankfully in the resolutions of an universe of force, and man unconsciously accepts his life in nature and his nature therefore from the same source, but, consciously, he knows no more of nature than he learns from his idealities of such realities; he does not see natures but only the images of natures reflected from his conscience of them,—as to the astronomer are stars and planets by his concave mirror,—and midway between impressions and the objects to produce them, and without the sense that his idealities are of the same cause as that of which are the realities that cause them;—he has the feeling that while nature, whatever that may be, is cause of the objective realities, he himself is cause of his subjective idealities, and of the volitions and activities they inspire, and of the families, stocks, tribes and states of man, therefore, into which he enters.

And the argument cannot now begin for the reason that I must make it in terms of reality, and man can accept it but in terms of his idealities; and in argument I must use the terms "being finite," "God," "force," "matter," "life," "nature," "universe," "star," "sun," "earth," "plant," "animal," "man," and "idealities," "families," "stocks," "tribes," and "states of man," as descriptive of realities objective in teleologic evo-involutions of an universe of force; while man must accept them but as descriptive of his idealities of these whose meanings are determined but as they have been agreed upon, with but a vague conception of the limits of such agreements. The argument therefore were not more interesting or intelligible than were an oration in Greek to an English audience. And to settle the grounds of argument in the definitions of terms I must give, and at even greater length, what may be termed an introduction. And I do this, however reluctantly, from the feeling that as there is occasion for this argument at all there is occasion for the preliminary statements necessary to its being understood, and these in definite indications of the differences there are between the terms of reality in which the argument is made and those of ideality in which it is received.

Upon the conscience of every individual man, itself a reality, there are the incidences of an universe of exterior realties, as upon the photographic plate there are incident in images the features of the landscape; and as the images are not the landscape, so the idealities are are not reality—to the subject of them at least; and these—not realities—are not even the same to different men, who therefore in discussions of them but beat the air. But the more of this unprofitable altercation must there be between him who speaks in terms of reality to him who hears in terms of ideality. Propositions in mathematics are conclusive for the reason that they are in terms of ideality the meanings of which have been fixed by definition; but propositions in physics are not conclusive for the reason that physics are realities, the terms of which in idealities have not only not been fixed by definition, but it is not realized that there are substantive realities susceptible of definition. There are realities but in the resolutions of an universe of force, and it is not seen, or agreed, at least, that there is such universe.

To the profound philosophy of Mr. Herbert Spencer himself in his evolution of nothing to evolve there is not the assertion of such reality as such nothing. He admits that there is reality, but a reality of whose substantive existence he has no conception sufficient for its definition. But affirming the substantive existence of reality of which I have conception as the noumenal cause of phenomenal consequences in force, the every one of which were the miracle of consequence without cause if there be not such cause, and presenting this as the condition of my theory of man at this earth in continuation of a nature of that universal reality in life throughout the universe, it is proper that in an introduction, however prolix, I give the meanings of the terms, being finite, God, the Word of God, force, space, matter, life, nature, universe, star, sun, earth, plant, animal, man, and stock, tribe and state of man, by which that theory may be expressed. This I propose to do in a further statement of intentions, which, appropriately or not, I term an introduction, and which, first as object lessons, will present the realities themselves in terms to which the definitions are to be applied.

INTRODUCTION.

SECTION I.

A PREFACE so extended might have been expected to protect the reader from further preliminary statement, but the point I make and the grounds I make it on are new; and as argument is waste without a clear perception by all parties of its subject, by way of further introduction I will say that this proposition is intended to present a theory of nature; and of man in nature, and of nature in the resolutions of a reality in life throughout the universe; and of man in continuation of that nature at this earth. And this the nature of the word of God in force; and this the nature of a general providence of life in nature to the takers of it possible; and these the stars, suns, planets, moons, meteorites, nebulæ and comets of the celestial sphere, and the forces, matters, plants, animals, man and idealities in man at this earth's surface.

It is intended that to man, at least, there is reality; that in man there is conscience, and that this in him is, as in the camera, the photographic plate to take the picture of the landscape. That as there are pictures on the plate, there are impressions upon conscience analogously the same; that these are idealities, no one of which were possible but of an objective reality incident to produce it; and that there are these objective realities, as, of these, in human conscience there are idealities subjective of them. Nor these only, but idealities themselves are realities when incident on conscience they occasion idealities. So that to every human conscience there is its environment of an universe of realities objective circumscribing an actual or potential universe of idealities subjective. The one of which objective realities were possible but as it be in tradition from an universal being in force of which in resolution there are the forces of this universe, which universe of force in such forces is reality.—And the one of which subjective idealities were possible but as it be in consequence of such objective reality in incidence to produce it. And that to man, therefore, there is reality for the reason that every instant of every instance of his consciousness is but of such reality in incidence upon his conscience to produce it, and that he is without the sense of reality but as he is without the sense of his existence.

And it is intended that of the reality there is nature. That of this as an universe of force,—the same as that of the physical forces, heat, light, electricity and magnetism, dynamic in that seeming vacuum we term space, and static in that apparent plenum we term matter,—there are forces different as are the minus and plus of electric force and the North and South of magnetic force and heat and light and electricity and magnetism. And, as such, that it is being physiological, that the being physiological is the being possible of kindred beings different of their reciprocal affinities simply in reciprocal limitations of each other. And that such is the moment of heat, light, electricity, or magnetism; and such the electro-magnetic spark; and such the magneto-electric spheroid proloblate; and such the molecule, compound or form of matter inorganic or organic; and such the earth, plant, animal or man—but the being possible of kindred beings different of their reciprocal affinities simply in reciprocal limitations of each other.

And it is intended that these beings are relatively dynamic and static and—of the same elements inversely—are reciprocally vacua and reciprocally plena, and reciprocally attractive and reciprocally repulsive, and of their reciprocal attractions are penultimately coincident on the line of their neutral being intermediate, and of their reciprocal repulsions are in penultimate differentiation from that line in production of the spheroid proloblate and wheel of the static being in revolution on its axis of the dynamic.

And that this wheel is in evo-involution—that the radiations of the axis in production of the disk is evolution, and the circumscription of the axis by the disk involution, and that the wheel is one of evo-involution. And that this evo-involution is teleologic—that the disk of every such wheel resolves into quadrants in each of which there are beings different in like reactions into a wheel in revolution on its axis and in its orbit of revolution on the parent axis, and so on to the wheels ultimately possible. And such the moment or medium of force it is intended that such is the universe of media. That this is being physiological in teleologic evo-involution, of which there are the stars, sun, earth, plant, and animal from that universe to man inclusive.

That of its beings different the dynamic is that which in beings about us we term life, and the static that in which such life appears which we term nature. And the universe of force, such wheel of which the axle is life and the disk nature, it is intended that with respect to such axis the disk of the universe in teleologic evo-involution is nature. And that thus of the reality there is nature.

And it is intended that of this nature there is man. That capable and cause of the sun, earth, plant and animal to man it were capable and cause of man, or at that point it were the miracle of cause without consequence. And man were the miracle of consequence without cause. And,—as man has never seen the miracle and cannot conceive the miracle,—to man there is not such miracle. And to man, therefore, of the reality there is nature and of nature man.

And it is intended that man in nature is in continuation of nature. And for the reason that man also is being physiological in teleological evo-involution—that of such evolution of the animal there is agamic man, and of agamic the polygamic man, and of the polygamic the monogamic man, and such evolution nature, that man is in continuation of nature.

And that he is in continuation of nature in continuing himself into the man possible and this the most and best man possible about this earth. And this for the reason that man is in nature at this earth from the resolutions of an universe of life in nature in every instance of which there is the life possible into its nature possible, and the life to man through the plant and animal can be satisfied but by such most and best man possible.

And intended that there is such man but in him of unequal races in relations of inequality, it is intended that man to such man is in continuation of a nature of reality throughout the universe, and that this is the nature of infinite being finite, and this the nature of the word of God in force, and this the nature of a general providence of life in nature to the takers of it possible, and these the stars and others of the celestial sphere and the plants and others at this earth.

And it is intended that this theory is true for the reason that the hypothesis of an universe of force is the induction of cause from consequence in phenomena of this universe and that the nature from the universe including man is the deduction simply from that hypothesis. And that the hypothesis were miracle without the phenomena of nature and the phenomena of nature were each the miracle if there be not that hypothesis.

And it is true for the further reason that it is the capitol and crowning generalization of terrestrial and celestial phenomena.

By Kepler it was found, from generalizations of celestial phenomena, that the planets move in ellipses, with the sun in one of their foci; each with its radius vector sweeping over equal areas in equal times and with the squares of their periodic times in proportion to the cubes of their mean distances.

And by Newton, in generalizations of terrestrial phenomena by the light of Kepler's laws, it was found that all bodies of matter at this earth are under the same laws of actual or potential motion to the earth's centre, expressed in gravitation, as are the planets to the central sun.

And—intended that these are the only important generalizations of phenomena to hypotheses and of consequence to cause and of nature to life and of man to God that have yet been made by man,—it is intended that forbearance of further generalization is gratuitous.

It is not true that God does not intend us to know his nature,—in that he has made its acceptance to us the condition of existence. Nor is it true as found by Kepler that planets so move in ellipses with the sun, but as they be beings physiological and in reciprocal limitations of each other, or these but as they be of the same elements inversely. Nor is it true as found by Newton that the matters at this earth's surface can so move in gravitations to its centre, but as the matters of the earth's crust and the space centre of the earth be in the same relations to each other as are the sun and planets and of the same elements inversely. This unification in substance of all phenomena subjective and objective solicits man's acceptance. It is the condition in fact of the uniformities of nature upon which the reason, science, knowledge, philosophy, religion and life of man depend. And accepting the uniformity we do in effect accept the condition of its existence, in accepting which we accept that there is man at this earth in continuation of a nature of reality throughout the universe to the man possible, and this the man of unequal races in relations of inequality.

And so true, it is further commended to acceptance in the fact that it presents to human sense another subject of human science. Man has now the science of phenomena but not of noumena, and of consequence but not of cause, and of nature but not of life. But in accepting this theory of an invisible universe of noumenon, cause, and life, into the visible universe of phenomena, consequences, and natures, we acquire a science of life as of nature and are no longer under the necessity of invoking the miracle we cannot realize to every nature coming into notice,—as even men of science do in requiring the miracle of consequence without cause in antecedent nature to the origin of every species of force, matter, plant, or animal.

And it is thus intended that of the reality there is nature, and of nature man, and that man of nature is in continuation of nature and to the man possible and to the man of unequal races contingent but upon the condition that there be reality.

And after this further statement of the proposition of man in continuation of nature it might be expected and desired by those who have been at pains to follow it so far that the argument begin. But still I am impelled to further preliminary statement. In looking over what is written so far I see the probability that the essential truth intended is not perceptible to the general reader. All that I have said or intend to say is in indication of the existence of an invisible and inconceivable reality, and this the being finite of beings infinite, and this the word of God's originating cause in terms of his own being, and this the force of forces opposite, reciprocal, and complementary, and this the noumenon of phenomena; and this the cause insensible of consequences sensible, and this the life invisible of natures visible, and this the conscience insensible of its own existence but as it is obliged to accept its existence as the cause of sensibilities otherwise the miracles of consequence without cause; and this that inconceivable being of which there is the calculus—integral in its life—and differential in its nature; and this that being to evolve, of which there are the evolutions of Mr. Spencer; and this that other than the anthropomorphic theos of theology, with respect to whose beings Mr. Huxley is content to be agnostic. And this that being intermediate life and nature, through which there are specific beings in forces, matters, plants and animals, which even scientists are willing to accept as the miracles of consequences without cause, the existence of which no single scientist is intellectually able to accept; and this that universal being the existence of which is established by inductions of universal phenomena no one of which were but the miracle of consequence without cause if it do not exist ; and this that being of life and nature of whose life there is, or is to be science, as there is of nature.

Intended that life is cause and nature consequence and that there is but life to nature and but nature to life, it is intended that of these two beings so conterminous the sense of one is the sense of the other, and the science of the one the science of the other, if man have intrepidity to accept it.

And such the being to the existence of which it is the purpose of the proposition to give recognition, it were manifestly vain to argue of its truth without perception of the truth intended, or to suppose that the conventional terms of the sciences of nature are sufficient to express the real terms of that being in life invisible of which only there is nature visible.

And upon a subject of so much importance, therefore, I must be indulged in the fullest statement possible as to its intentions, and that there is reality, and that of this there is nature, and of nature man, and that man of nature is in continuation of nature, and this but in being his most and best.

Section II.

True if there be Reality.

Such the theory of man in continuation of nature, it is intended that it is true if there be reality : That if there be reality there is nature; and if there be nature there is man in nature; and if there be man in nature he is in continuation of nature contingent but upon the condition that there be reality.

Intended that if there be reality it is the being finite of the word of God in force; that this is being physiological; that this is in teleologic evo-involution; that such resolution of reality is nature in successive natures; and that of such resolution of the universal reality in force there are the stars, sun, earth, plant, and animal, each a nature from the universe to man inclusive,—it is intended that of the reality there is nature; and for the reason that the reality is capable of nature, and nature possible of reality; and that of nature there is man for the reason that nature is capable of man, and man possible of nature; and that man of nature is consequence of nature and in continuation of nature as is consequence of cause.

And that the reality is capable of nature and as being, simply, capable; and as infinite being finite capable; and as the word of God capable; and as force capable,—in that, whether as being, simply, or infinite being finite, or the word of God, or force it were being physiological,—the being possible of

INTRODUCTION. 39

kindred beings different of their reciprocal affinities simply in reciprocal limitations of each other in production of the being of both on its axis of the one, and this in teleologic evo-involution. That such evo-involution were into the beings possible in revolutions on their axis, and in orbits of revolution on their parent axis. And capable of this that it were capable of nature.

And that it were so capable, it is intended that whether as being simply or as infinite being finite or the word of God or force, the reality were the being possible of kindred beings different of their affinities simply in limitations of each other. That there is being simply but as it be of beings indefinitely large and indefinitely small in reciprocal contradictions of each other; or infinite being finite but as these infinites be opposites and reciprocally contradictory; or the word of God in such the finite of his beings infinite; or force but as it be being and infinite being finite and the word of God, such, and but as it be this in the physical forces, heat, light, electricity and magnetism dynamic in that seeming vacuum we term space, and static in that apparent plenum we term matter.

And that these such beings are in reciprocal limitations of each other, but as they be in penultimate coincidence and differentiation on the axis of their neutral being intermediate, that they are so but as they be reciprocally attractive and reciprocally repulsive; and so but as they be reciprocally vacua and reciprocally plena; and so but as they be of the same elements of being and of these inversely.

But so related,—as are the minus and plus of electricity, or heat and light, or electricity and magnetism, or space and matter, or the negative and positive atoms of the matter molecule, or the acid and base of the matter compound, or the staminate and pistillate of the plant, or the sperm and germ, or male and female principles of the animal,—that, of the same elements inversely, they are of their unlike elements reciprocally vacua and attractive, and of their like elements reciprocally plena and repulsive, and of their reciprocal attractions in penultimate coincidence on the line as axis of their neutral being intermediate, and of their reciprocal repulsions in penultimate differentiation thence in production of the spheroid proloblate of prolate and oblate spheroids,—the one spindle and the other spool,—and this a wheel physiological of both in revolution on its axis of the one.

It is intended that beings so related are dynamic and static in their special beings relatively; and the one fast and the other slow; and that in coincidence and differentiation,—the one is screw and the other nut,—the screw to enter and disrupt the nut and project it in rays of screw and nut into such spheroid of both in revolution on its axis of the one; which axle is of the one being prepotent and its disk of the other, and its spokes of both alternately prepotent to sustain the disk and axle in relation.

INTRODUCTION. 41

And,—such the being physiological of which the reality is capable,—it is intended that of this there is teleologic evo-involution.

It is intended that every such wheel is a medium of reality and,—this of such kindred beings different,—that in this of such beings different there are their reciprocal inductions, and through these their self-insulations, self-differentiations and coincidences and differentiations in production of the wheel physiological of both on its axis of the one.

But that the disk of that wheel is a medium, also, not essentially different from the original media and in form different but as it be in a disk of relatively being static about its included axis of being dynamic. And that of the reciprocal inductions of the beings different of such disk there are its self-insulations into four parts, each a quadrant of the disk and each a medium in self-insulation, self-differentiation, coincidence and differentiation into a peripherential wheel physiological in revolution on its individual axis and in orbits of revolution on the parent axis.

And such the theoretical reality physiological, it is intended that such is the actual being physiological from every medium of force. It is intended that every such physiological reality in force,—whether as the moment of heat, light, electricity or magnetism, or as the spark of these in heat and light, or as the spheroid proloblate of these in magnetic moments about their axis of electrical reactions, itself producing the disk of magnetic moments, themselves producing the electrical axis in reactions to produce them,—is an **autonomy**; and this a self-existing, automatic, autonomic, teleologic universal one and only being of this universe. And that each itself, such automony, is of infinitesimal autonomies—each such wheel physiological of but two atomic finites of their reciprocal affinities in reactions of coincidence and differentiation on their axis of neutral being intermediate; that of these ultimate atomic finites the one is the original of that dynamic being we see as the minus of electric force, and the other of that static being we see as the plus, and that the one is the original of that we see as heat and the other of that we see as light; and that the one is electricity and the other magnetism; and the one cause and the other consequence; and the one life and the other nature.

And it is intended that each such force of these is an autonomy, for the reason that it is of no force *ab extra*, but simply an existence in force, exclusive of other such beings from the reciprocal affinities in attraction and repulsion of the beings,—atomic of their reciprocal inductions,—involved.

It is intended that any two infinitesimal realities in force both of the same beings different are of their unlike elements reciprocally attractive, and of their like elements reciprocally repulsive; that in this they are reciprocally inductive of each other; and of their attractions meet on the axis of their neutral being intermediate with but their reciprocal repulsion to resist such meeting; and of their reciprocal repulsions, part from such axis with but their reciprocal attractions to prevent such parting. That under operation of such four elements of being different these form in the disk of a wheel about such axis,—from their attractions being under the conditions greater than their repulsions; and,—of their superior attractions clinging to such axis,—that of their superior repulsions they exclude and project from such nucleus all other beings not so involved and establish, within, a consensus of individuality conservative of its individual existence and obstructive and destructive of all other beings adjacent to disturb it,—but as they be forming in the disk of such wheel physiological and in concurrence with it in production of a larger wheel in every way but in size the same as the original. That thus there are accretions in opposite directions from such original axis of such original disk, and that each such accretion is analogous to the continuous reproduction of the animal or plant, but to become discontinuous with increasing distance from the axis; that in this there is waning attachments of peripherential beings to the parent axis, and a waxing attachment to the local axis of their own; and that in this there is the enlargement of the disk of the wheel physiological and the resolution of that disk into peripherential wheels in revolution on their axis, and in orbits of revolution on their parent axis. And intended that coincidence is involution and differentiation evolution and the resolution of the parent disk into progenital wheels the being teleologic, it is intended that this process of the parent wheel into progenital wheels possible is teleologic evo-involution. And intended that of the reality there is an universe, it is intended that of this in evo-involution there are stars about the axis of the universe, and suns about the axis of stars, and planets about the axis of suns; and that about the axis of this earth, a planet in evo-involution, there are the molecular matters of its crust, and at its surface the compounds of these, and the plants of these, and the animal of these, and the man of these in continuation simply of this earth's process of teleologic evo-involution. And intended that such teleologic evo-involution of reality is nature, it is intended that this reality capable of this is capable of nature. And intended that there is a nature through stars, sun, earth, plant and animal from the universe to man inclusive, and that these are beings finite of being infinite; it is intended that of this nature the universal reality as being finite is capable. And intended that there is a nature of God from the universe to man inclusive; it is intended that of this nature the reality as the word of God is capable. And intended that there is a nature of force from the universe to man, it is intended that of this nature the reality, as the universe of force, is capable.

It is intended that if there be dynamic force sufficient on matter it is sublimed to space in heat and light; and if there be static force sufficient it is reduced to space in cold and dark, the heat and light representing the minus and plus of electricity, and the cold and dark the north and south of magnetism; and that minus is space to plus matter, and heat space to light matter, and south space to north matter, and electricity space to magnetism matter; and that in each of these reactions there is the being physiological in teleologic evo-involutions of reality, as there are in the star, sun, earth, plant and animal from the universal reality of infinite being finite and the word of God to man; and that thus the reality were capable of nature and capable were cause. And this in that to conscious man capability is cause; that whatever be the fact, man is conscious of an universe of cause to an universe of consequence and of an universe of consequence to an universe of cause; that he has not seen nor can he conceive of an instance of cause without consequence or of consequence without cause; that his axioms, reason, knowledge, religion, and life itself, are upon the condition of an universe of cause to an universe of consequence and of an universe of consequence to an universe of cause, the contrary of which were the miracle of factors without product or product without factors he has not seen and cannot see; so that, if the reality capable be not cause of nature, there is in such reality the miracle of cause without consequence; and in such nature, then possible of the reality, the miracle of consequence without cause: since, than the exclusive universe of reality, there is nothing else to cause the universe of nature and in the exclusive universe of nature there is nothing else but nature to consequence the universal reality.

And it is intended that for like reason of nature there is man; that nature in teleologic evo-involution of an universal reality is capable of man and man possible of such nature; and, capability cause and possibility consequence, that nature were cause of man and man consequence of nature without the miracles of cause without consequence or consequence without cause; and without the even greater miracle there were in a nature and a man in nature of an anthropomorphic theos of his own imagination. And intended that there is not such miracle, it is intended that if there be reality there is nature, and man in nature, and man in continuation of nature; and that there is man in continuation of a nature of reality, and that thus there is the nature of a reality in life throughout the universe and man in continuation of that nature, contingent but upon the condition that there be reality. And this the nature of infinite being finite, and this the nature of the word of God, and this the nature of an universe of force in teleologic evo-involution, and this the nature of the infinite God and not of an anthropomorphic theos, and this the nature of religion and not of theology in the superstitions of an earlier man; and a nature in science of which there is also the science of life.

Intended that nature is of life and nature, and that so is man of life and nature and so the conscience of man, it is intended that the life of conscience is perceptive but of the nature of objective being as the eye sees its object but not itself; and that in man it is the photographic plate to take the pictures of the natures of the landscape visible but not of their lives invisible; and that there is but empirical science, and this but of objects visible; and science but of nature therefore. But from the universal truth of cause to consequence and consequence to cause,—that the science of nature is in effect the science of life; that so related as are these, the representatives to us, of the beings infinite of whose limitations of each other there is the word of God in force,—there is not life without nature or nature without life; or life but as the being of the most of life to the least of nature, and nature but as the being of the most of nature and the least of life. And it is intended that as there is consciously the science of nature, there is unconsciouly the science of life, to become consciously the science of life when man shall have the intellectual intrepidity to accept and entertain that invisible cause of consequences visible, not one of which were possible but as there be such cause.

It is intended that these life and nature are as cause and consequence, and noumena and phenomena; and that as there is an actual science of phenomena there is a possible science of noumena, and that in the meantime, and before man shall sensibly accept such science of life by deduction from the hypothesis established by induction of the phenomena, he must, as the condition of every act of his physical or moral being, intuitively and scientifically accept that life without which the everything in nature were the miracle of consequence without cause ; and intended that the life of science is the life of reason, and that the life not of science is a life of superstition, and that reason is of God, and superstition of the anthropomorphic theos in the place of God, and that the culture of God is religion and the culture of theos theology, it is intended that this nature of reality of which man is in continuation at this earth is the nature of cause as of consequence, and of space invisible as of matter visible, and of life insensible as of nature sensible, and of religion in obedience to the real God of this universe in force, instead of theology in obedience to the imaginary and anthropomorphic theos of human superstition. And that there is this nature if there be reality for the reason that nature were else the miracle without, and man of nature if there be nature, and man in continuation of nature from being consequence of cause in nature, which can be but in continuation of its cause, and that the theory is true if there be reality.

Section III.

That there is Reality.

It is intended that there is reality and this in the being finite of the word of God in force; and this the original self-existent, automatic, autonomic, teleologic one and only being of this universe. That there is being finite of beings infinite in reciprocal limitations of each other; and the word of God in such the finite of his beings infinite; and force in the physical forces, heat, light, electricity, magnetism,—dynamic in that seeming vacuum we term space, and static in that apparent plenum we term matter,—and but in phenomena to conscience of that finite word. And that of this there is an universe and,—as the being finite of beings infinite,—an universe; and,—as the word of God the universal cause,—an universe; and as force in phenomena of that universal word, an universe; and as force,—the universe of which were the condition of every instance of force at any point of time or place,—an universe. And this at any point of place or time, within this universe; or whether as being infinite, or finite, simply,—or as the being finite of beings infinite in reciprocal limitations of each other, or as the word of God; or as force; or as the moment or medium of thermal, photal, electric or magnetic force, or as the moment or medium of space; or as the atom, molecule, compound, or form of matter inorganic or organic in plant, animal, or man,—is being original, in that it is without previous existence at its time and place as such; and self-existent in its consistence, but of its own beings in reaction; and automatic in its activities but of its own means; and autonomic in its activities but to its own ends; and teleologic in its evo-involution of parent into progeny; and universal for the reason stated. And that it is the one and only being of this universe, in that, than this, as being infinite, or finite, simply, there is no other; and as the being finite of beings infinite,—no other; and as the word of God the universal cause,—no other; and as force, but in phenomena of that word,—no other; and as force, the instance of which were possible, but as there be an exclusive universe of force,—no other. And that this is that being of which there are the objective beings incident in stars and planets of the celestial sphere, and forces and matters inorganic and organic at this earth; and that these are all of this one and only being of the word of God in force. And that this is that being of which in man there is the subjective consciousness of such objective beings; that in man, himself objective being, there is being termed his conscience, and that this as such, in man, is as in the camera the photographic plate prepared to take the picture of the landscape; that as of a something from the landscape in incidence upon a something in the plate there is a picture on the plate, so of a something from objective being in incidence upon a something in conscience there is ideality in being of that objective being to produce it; and that this ideality in conscience is being; and this the same as that of objective being to produce it; and that conscience itself is being; and this the same as that of objective being to affect it. That to such sense in conscience of its object there is reaction between the beings of conscience and its object, and that there is this but as the essential beings of conscience and its object be in coincidence and differentiation upon the axis of their neutral being intermediate; that there is this but as these beings be reciprocally attractive and reciprocally repulsive; that they are so but as they be reciprocally vacua and reciprocally plena; that they are so but as they be of the same elements inversely; and that thus there is being objective and subjective and these essentially the same. And that this is that being in force of which there are the forces of this universe.

It is intended that of *moderate* force, dynamic or static on matter, at rest or in motion, there are expressed the forces heat, light, electricity and magnet ism; and that of *immoderate* force, dynamic or stati on matter, there is its disappearance as matter an. its reappearance in force of heat, light, electricit\ or magnetism; that these forces are but the phenomenal phases of the essential being, force, and that this is the objective and subjective finite word of God; and that this is that being in space of which there are the spaces of this universe. Intended that of force on matter there are the physical forces, but in states of intensity invisible; and that matter therefore is visible but in its solid, liquid and gaseous states; and in its innumerable other states invisible, as is that seeming vacuum between matters we term space; it is intended that for this reason there is the essential substance of that apparent plenum we term matter in the interval between matters; and that in these intervals there are beings invisible reacting with matters, but as matters invisible could react with matters visible; and that there is an invisible universe of space as real as the planetary orbs of matter in it; and that these realities in matter are in proportion to their reciprocal reality, invisible in space as are the planets of this solar system to their orbits, and as are the motes upon the sunbeam to the sunbeam on which they float; and that this is that being in matter of which there are the matters of the universe.

Intended that there are stars, suns, planets, moons, meteorites, nebulæ, and comets of the celestial sphere, and at this earth a planet, plants, animals, men and idealities in men; and that these are all of that static being visible we term matter, and that this is of that relatively dynamic of which we are sensible as force; it is intended that, as of force infused into matter there is matter raised to space, so of force withdrawn from space there is space reduced to matter, as daily of heat withdrawn from this earth's atmosphere of force there is the fall of water forming in it; that of such rains or snows there is no other source ; that the waters falling from the clouds do not rise in vapor but in heat; that there was once a time when there was not water, or hydrogen, or any non-metallic element of matter save oxygen in existence at the earth's surface to rise from it, and as waters fell then more abundantly than they fall now and but from heat, that they fall now but from heat condensed to water from reaction with this exterior atmosphere of force in cold. And that this being is reality and as the substance of objective beings reality; and as the cause of idealities reality; and as being finite reality; and as the word of God reality; and as force reality; and as the cause of life reality; and of nature reality; and of the stars, sun, earth, plant, animal and man,—realities,—reality.

It is intended that there are two modes of the reality different, and the one energy and the other inertia, and the one dynamic and the other static, and the one life and the other nature in reactions of coincidence and differentiation; that of these two modes of being there are the beings of this universe to man, and that these beings are natures in a course of nature from the universe to man; and that of these natures the reality is cause, and of this course of nature it is cause, and that of the life of which there is nature it is cause; that the reality is of beings different in that they are of the same elements inversely, and that these are reciprocally vacua and reciprocally plena, and reciprocally attractive and reciprocally repulsive, and of such their affinities that they are in coincidence and differentiation in production of the wheel physiological of both in teleologic evo-involution; and that this is nature, and that of this there are the natures of the universe and the course of such natures from the universe to man. And these natures reality and the cause reality, it is intended that the cause of the life of which there are these natures is reality, and of the natures and the course of natures reality, to man at least, who must accept that as reality upon which his consciousness and existence both depend.

Intended that there is an universe but of cause to consequence and consequence to cause, and that man is of such universe and his conscience of such universe, and that this conscience is of cause to consequence and consequence to cause, and can realize being or the being or beings of this universe but as they be of cause to consequence and consequence to cause, it is intended that capability is cause and that the reality capable of nature is cause of nature, and that to man there is reality if to man it rationally appear that there is that in existence which could not be without reality and that there are such beings; that there is this solar system possible but of the evo-involution of an universal reality in force; and this earth possible but of the evo-involution of a solar medium of reality; and the successive strata of this earth's crust possible but of the earth's medium of reality in evo-involution; and this earth's atmosphere of force possible but of radiations of reality, from the surface of the earth, in evo-involution.

It is intended that exterior to the earth's surface of water there is its atmosphere of force physiological apparent in the fact that if there be disturbance of it at any point about the earth by artificial force there is the resolution of that disturbance into beings physiological. That such are the beings in heat, light, electricity, and magnetism, and systems of these from force on matter; and such sound, and the subjects of touch, taste, smell and sight; and such the messages delivered by the telegraph and telephone. It is intended that every such message were the miracle of consequence without cause if there be not an atmosphere of force physiological to register at one point the changes made by force upon it at another, and that such is the plant's atmosphere of force physiological possible but of radiations of reality from the plant in evo-involution.

It is intended that exterior to the plant in its variations to its beings possible there is an atmosphere actual or potential of force physiological through which of its radiating energy the plant is formed into the plant possible; and that such is the animal atmosphere of force physiological through which there is at every stage of its process the animal possible, and of the radiate the annulate, and of the annulate the articulate, and of the articulate the vertebrate, and of the vertebrate the fish, and of the fish the reptile, and of this the digitigrade, and of this the plantigrade, and of this the four-handed, and of this the two-footed and two-handed animal. And that such is the human atmosphere of force physiological termed civilization, through ministrations of which in making man the man possible there are successively agamic, polygamic and monogamic man, and through which there is to be the man compounded of an union of unequal races in relations of inequality. And that such is the medium of values in every human civilization termed money—the same to man in polar relations of supply and want to each other as is the force electric or magnetic between the poles of the battery or magnet. And that such generally is the being finite or the word of God, or force, or the moment of thermal, photal, electric, or magnetic force, or the moment of space, or the molecule compound, or form of matter inorganic or organic, plant, animal, or man or ideality in man, not one of which were possible, or but the miracle of consequence without cause, if there be not reality in the finite word of God in force; that such also were life, nature, and in man the ideality of such reality. And that there is reality therefore as there be the sun, earth, or atmosphere of force physiological, or God or the word of God, or being finite, or force, or the moment of force, or space, or the moment of space, or matter, or the molecule compound or form of matter, inorganic or organic, or in plant, animal, or man, or as there be life or nature, or a thing of nature, or in man the sense of the one of these. And intended that there is not only the one but the every one of these, it is intended that there is reality. But a reality of which in man there is not and cannot be objective sense; and, for reason that it is itself that being in man through which there is the sense of his own being and of beings with him, and, —itself man's conscience—that this conscience can see itself but as the eye in seeing objects can see itself; that the eye in seeing objects can see inductively that in doing this it must itself exist as a being susceptible of such sensations, but only as the possible hypothesis of such phenomena; that as such reality it is infinite being finite, and of life infinite into nature finite, and as such an original self-existent, automatic and teleologic autonomy in being simply of the word of God's own being in life into the natures of it possible—and such reality, that there is reality as there are the realities, the one of which were not possible without it.

Section IV.

That of the Reality there is Nature.

SUCH reality in the original self-existent, automatic, autonomic, teleologic universal one and only being finite of the word of God in force; it is intended that of this there is nature in that this is capable of nature, and, capability cause, the cause of nature. And in that there is nature possible of reality; and possibility consequence the consequence of reality. And that the reality is capable of nature in that it is being physiological; that being physiological is the being possible of kindred beings different of their reciprocal affinities simply in reciprocal limitations of each other; that this in form of a spheroid proloblate of prolate and oblate spheroids, the one spindle and the other spool,—the spool in revolution on its axle of the spindle, and this in evo-involution of the spool into such spheroids of relative matter in revolutions on their axes, and in orbs and in orbits of revolution on their parent axis of included space. And that this resolution of such beings different into such wheel physiological of spindle and spool is nature, and that this of the spool by evo-involution into wheels in revolution on their axes and in orbits on the parent axis is also nature; and that as being simply it is so capable and as being finite capable; and as the word of God capable and as force capable. And as being simply capable.

It is intended that whether there be specifically the being finite, or the word of God, or force, there is at least, to conscious man, the ultimate term of organic matter at this earth,—being. There is in man being; and in the conscience of man being; and in the objective beings in incidence upon subjective conscience,—being; and that such being simply is being physiological, and so capable of nature.

It is intended that there is being infinite or finite; or both infinite and finite; and infinite in the elements of being involved; and finite in the limitations of the one infinite by another infinite as itself; but that to us there is the conception of such being but as it be midway between infinites large and small, and but as these be in reaction from their polar states of being invisible to produce it intermediate, as the neutual being intermediate, the poles of the battery or magnet; and but as it be in modes of being, the one from the inconceivably small to the inconceivably large, and as the other be from the inconceivably large to the inconceivably small, and the one from nothing to infinity and the other from infinity to nothing; and but as this being conceivable be of beings different, opposite, reciprocal, and complementary; and but as the ones be from small to large and the others from large to small; and as the ones be from centre to surface and the others from surface to centre, and as the ones be centrifugal and the others be centripetal; and as the ones be radical and the others peripherential; and but as in every radiation of such being from its axis, and in every peripherential line of such being about its axis there be beings opposite; and in reaction in every such ray and line; and on every point of such ray and line, and on every point in coincidence and differentiation in production of the wheel physiological of both on its axis of the one; and this in teleologic evo-involution and that this is being physiological, and that thus in being simply there is being physiological.

And such infinite, or finite, being simply that such the more certainly is infinite being finite; that there is being finite but of beings infinite in reciprocal limitations of each other,—possible but as they be attractive and repulsive, reciprocally,—possible but as they be reciprocally vacua and plena,—possible but as they be of the same elements inversely, but that so related and in any medium they are in such coincidence on the line, as axis, of their neutral being intermediate; and as screw and nut in production of the spheroid and wheel physiological of both, the axle of which is in potency of the one being infinite, and the disk of the other; and the spokes of both, alternately prepotent, to sustain the disk and axle in relation; and that this finite the being possible of kindred beings different, of their reciprocal affinities, simply, in reciprocal limitations of each other,—is being physiological.

And that this, as the word of God is being physiological. That there is God but as cause; and cause but through means; and through means but of his own infinite beings finite; and finite but in their reciprocal limitations of each other,—possible but of their coincidences and differentiations,—of their reciprocal affinities in production, on the. axis intermediate of the spheroid and wheel of both in revolution on its axis of the one. And this the being finite of the beings infinite; and that being physiological,—that the word of God is being physiological. And this,—the possible of beings different of their affinities simply in limitations of each other,—is being physiological.

And that this, as force, but in phenomena of that noumenal reality in the finite word of God is being physiological. And that this,—as force, the cause invisible of consequences visible in heat, light, electricity, magnetism, space and matter is such, and that each of these is such being physiological.

It is intended that if there be *moderate* force physical, or chemical, on matter solid or liquid insulated, there are produced at its extremities the electric forces minus and plus, and these in atomic. and polar relations to each other upon the available line, as axis, of their neutral being; and that these, when in sufficient quantity, react sensibly upon that line; and,—if unconducted,—into the spark of heat ard light, and,—if conducted,—into the spheroid proloblate and wheel of magnetic moments moving about this line as axis of electrical elements reacting to produce them. But it is intended that if there be *immoderate* force, physical or chemical, in matter solid or liquid, or insulated or uninsulated,—as if there be the incidence of a ball, of even platinum upon another in velocity of the planet; or whatever the velocity; in force of this earth's planetary weight; or if it be projected, merely, in velocity of light; or if upon it there be a beam of heat in intensity sufficient; or through it a current of electricity—in quantity sufficient, it is instantly sublimed to heat and light. Or if upon the same ball there be immoderate static force,—as were that of a cold of minus 1,000° F., or that of the weight, without motion, of this earth, or that of a light, or magnetism the intensest possible, it were as instantly dissipated and occluded in a medium of invisible being such as is that between matters acting at a distance.

It is intended that there are stars in couples; and the sun and earth and the eye and its distant object and bodies of matter in attractions, repulsions and gravitations of each other; that these are all matters acting at a distance, whose reciprocal activities were the miracles of consequences without cause if there be not intermediate an invisible being of the same essential substance, in reacting with which they are, in effect, reacting with each other. And it is intended that this substance, the product of matter under static force, is the same as that in phenomena of heat and light the product of matter under force dynamic; and that the existence of either, as such product, is sufficient to establish that all matter, metallic or non-metallic, or basic or acid, or inorganic or organic, is of the same essential substance, and the same as that of force, and that the substance of all forces, physical, chemical, physiological, psycological or sociological, are essentially the same; that the inordinate dynamic forces of impact, pressure, projection, heat and electricity, in producing all kinds of matter into heat and light, are the same essentially as are those of cold or pressure simply, or light or magnetism, which produce it into cold and dark, and that this one, and only universal force, whether as the being or the word of God, or as a being self-existent, automatic, autonomic and unique, is the being possible of kindred beings different of their reciprocal affinities simply through reciprocal limitations of each other in production of the being intermediate of both ; that such are the electromagnetic moments of heat visible in light from coincidence and differentiation of the dynamic forces in impact, pressure, projection, heat or electricity ; and such the magneto-electric moments of darkness sensible in cold from the coincidence and differentiation of static forces in cold, pressure, light and magnetism. That these forces, dynamic or static, essentially the same, are different in appearance merely, and,—but the phenomenal phases of an original and insensible reality,—are different but as our senses to perceive them ; that our senses are sight, touch, taste, smell and hearing; that these are but the points of the incidences of exterior realities upon the conscious being of man ; that this,—a wheel physiological in reactions of potential coincidence and differentiation with exterior realities, is susceptive of impressions in touch, taste, smell and hearing at four points of its periphery in revolution on its axis in the sense of sight to which they report, and which therefore is the systemic sense of these specific in determining the conscious activities of man; but that whatever our senses of such exterior reality, or whether we see it as being in force, dynamic or static, or as heat or cold; or as light, or dark, or as electricity, or magnetism, or space, or matter, or as the molecule, compound, form or organism of matter, or as star, sun, earth, plant, animal or man, it is the being possible of kindred beings different of their reciprocal affinities simply in reciprocal limitations of each other. That such is the moment of heat from the more of minus electricity to the less of plus; and such the moment of light from its more of plus to less of minus and the electric moment of more of heat to less of light; and the magnetic moment of more of light to less of heat; and the acid matter molecule from its more of electricity to its less of magnetism; and the basic matter from its more of magnetism to its less of electricity.

And that so is the staminate principle of the plant dynamic to its pistillate static; and so the sperm and male principle of the animal dynamic to the germ and female static; and so the parent of the human family dynamic to the progeny static; and so the centre of the earth dynamic to its crust static; and so

INTRODUCTION. 65

the centre of sun dynamic to its crust static; and so the crusts and centres of the stars and universe.

It is intended that each of these beings in force is mediately or immediately from an original medium of force physiological, and that each is itself a medium of force physiological however evo-involved from its original state; that in each there are self-insulation, self-differentiation, coincidence and differentiation analogously such as are these in that medium of force between electrodes, from which of electric forces, self-insulated, self-differentiated, and in coincidence and differentiation there is unconducted the spark of heat and light, or conducted the magneto-electric spheroid of magnetic moments about the axis of electrical reactions. And that such are the reactions of the like forces in the intervals of clouds in polar relations to each other; and that analogously such are the reactions between inorganic matters and organic matters, and the physiological elements of plants, animals and man the being possible of such elements reacting. And it is intended that every such being possible is the being physiological, and that every such is in a wheel of its static elements in revolution on their axis of the dynamic. That these elements of being physical, chemical, physiological, psycological, or sociological are beings of the same elements, and of these elements inversely; that so they are vacua and plena, and attractive and repulsive, and in coincidence and differentiation in production of such wheel physiological of both; and that thus the reality, whether as being simply; or as the being finite of beings infinite in limitations of each other; or the word of God in such the finite of his beings infinite; or force in the physical forces, heat, light, electricity and magnetism, or matter metallic or non-metallic, or acid or base, inorganic or organic, is the being possible of kindred beings different of their reciprocal affinities simply in reciprocal limitations of each other, and as such is being physiological.

And that of this there is teleologic evo-involution. That, as in every original medium of this being, invisible or visible, or of space or matter, or of matter inorganic or organic, there are its self-insulation, self-differentiation, coincidence and differentiation in production of such wheel physiological, so in the disk of such wheel there are media in every way but in sizes and densities the same as the original medium. That in every such disk there are normally four such media, each a quadrant of such disk, in each of which, for the same reason, there are self-insulation, self-differentiation, coincidence and differentiation in production of wheels physiological in revolution on their individual axes and in orbits of revolution on the parent axis. And intended that the revolutions of the axis of every such parent wheel in production is evolution, and resolutions of the disk in production of the axis of peripherential and progenital wheels is involution, and that this process of the parent wheel into progenital wheels and of parent life into parent nature is teleologic, it is intended that such process is one of teleologic evo-involution. And—this nature—that thus there is reality capable of nature; and capability cause—the cause of nature. And it is intended that of the reality there is nature for the further reason that there is a nature possible of reality; and—possibility consequence—the consequence of reality.

It is intended that about the invisible axis of the universe there are stars in crusts of relative matters invisible or visible about centres of relative space invisible, and about these as centres suns such, and about these as centres planets such; of which at its physiological distance from the axis of the universe there is this earth a planet in its crust of matter visible about its centre of space invisible. The crust in hollow spherical strata, the first of which is of platano-metallic matter, about which there is such stratum of metallic oxide matter in archean rocks; about which there is such stratum of hydrogens oxide in water liquid; about which there is an atmosphere of force in 60° F. of heat under a pressure in cold of 15 pounds to the inch, from which in vapor there are forming other hydrogens oxide; from vapors of which there are forming viscid and protoplasmic ammonias compound; of which are forming plants possible, of which are forming animals possible, of which are forming man possible. And intended that in the space centre of the universe there is the cause invisible of its crusts of stars, suns and planets—consequences—visible; and that in the space centres of stars there are the causes invisible of their crusts and suns, consequences visible, and in the space centres of suns the causes of these crusts and planets; and that in the space centre of this earth the cause of its platanic crust, the cause of its archean rock crust, the cause of its liquid water crust, the cause of its protoplasmic crust, the cause of its plant crust, the cause of its animal crust, the cause of its man crust,—it is intended that these actual or theoretical space centres are analogously the same and the causes invisible of their consequences visible, and the lives invisible of their natures visible; that in this there is a process of life and nature from the axis of the universe, and that this process visible of life invisible is nature and that there is nature. And intended that each such nature is the wheel physiological of forces different of their reciprocal affinities simply in reciprocal limitations of each other; and that of this the space centre is axle and the matter crust disk, and the invisible life centre axle and the matter corpus disk, it is intended that each such nature is possible of an universal reality in evo-involution. And that capability is cause and possibility consequence.

Intended that truth is that which man must accept as the condition of his existence in nature, and that, —of nature,—he is of the evo-involutions of an invisible reality teleologic in plant, animal and man at this earth's surface, in conscience of whom is the instrument through which he sees the universe of nature apparent; it is intended that at his time and place posterior to the animal at this earth's surface there is in him but the energy and inertia, and cause and consequence, and life and nature possible to him at such time and place of an universal reality in evo-involution. And,—but this to man himself,—there is but this to the conscience of man, the moral principle of his being under the conditions physically possible. That analogously such is that of the star, sun and earth, through moral ministrations of which each at its time and place is the being physically possible, and that of the plant or animal through which that is the being possible. That through this there is antecedent life into antecedent nature possible, and through this there is the life possible to man into the nature possible. That in this, such moral principle can accept but cause to consequence and consequence to cause, and but life to nature and nature to life, and can apply to nature but the life it receives, and that so only can the conscious moral principle of man,—whose axioms, reason, science, knowledge, religion, and life itself depend upon the exact limitation of cause to consequence, and consequence to cause, and life to nature, and nature to life,—apply to man or nature the life it is able to receive.

And such the relation of conscious man to the being of this universe, it is intended that he has not seen cause but to consequence or consequence but to cause, and that he cannot conceive the cause of other or more or less than consequence, or consequence of other or more or less than cause. And,— that truth to man which he must accept as true to the continuation of his existence,—and that truth of which he cannot conceive to the contrary, it is intended that it is truth to man whatever be the fact that there is to him an universe of consequence to an universe of cause; that these are as factors to product and product to factors. That in these capability is cause and possibility consequence; and that the reality capable of nature is cause of nature, and nature possible of reality is consequence of reality. And it is intended that not only is this necessary truth to man, but that he unconsciously and consciously accepts it as true in the laws of physics, chemistry, physiology and sociology, of which he is in practice to the continuation of his existence and in consciously making it the rule of every mental process.

The clown or idiot, equally with the sage, is an encyclopedia of truth, the title-page of which he cannot, or can but, read. And the young mother forms to exquisite symmetry her babe, not one hair of whose head or nail of whose finger could she intelligently make if the life of her infant, dearer than her own, depended on it. And so unconsciously accepting the truth of an universe of cause to an universe of consequence, man consciously accepts that truth in his every act of reason, science, knowledge, or philosophy.

It is thus intended that there is nature of reality in the reason that the reality is capable of nature and nature possible of reality; and it is intended that to man, at least, there is the nature of reality; for the reason that if to him there be nature at all it is of reality; for the reason stated. And that to him there is nature in that there is that which could not be without it. That of these is the being finite, or the word of God, or force, or space, or matter, or life, or nature, or of nature the universe, or star, or sun, or earth, or plant, or animal, or man, or the conscience, family stock, tribe or state of man, no one of which were possible but as there be nature in evo-involution of the word of God in force. And that there is nature of reality for the reason that to man there is nature but as it be of the reality, and that for reason that to man there is nature of reality there is in truth a nature of reality, and for the reason that rationally there is nature of reality. That by induction of the phenomena of nature there is the hypothesis of reality; and by deduction from the hypothesis of reality there are the phenomena of nature. That in induction and deduction there is reason; that reason is conclusive upon man's belief, and that whether by reason of induction or deduction there is to man the truth that there is reality, and that there is nature, and that of the reality there is nature. And for the reason that the reality were cause, and that without this there is no cause save that in the anthropomorph of man's imagination, which, not the cause of man himself, is not the cause of the earth and universe. And for these reasons that of the reality there is nature, whether there be man in that nature of reality or not.

Section V.

That of Nature there is Man.

INTENDED thus that of the reality there is nature, whether that be inclusive of man in matter at this earth or not; it is intended that it is inclusive, and this for the reason that man himself is of that teleologic evo-involution of reality of which are the natures of the universe to man, and each of these a nature,— that man is a nature. And intended that the course of the reality in life from the universe is nature, it is intended that man of that course is of that nature, whether in continuation of that nature or not. And that man is of that course. Intended that there is nature in the reaction of polar beings finite; that such are the elements minus and plus of electric force, and south and north of magnetic force; and heat, and light, and electricity, and magnetism, and the staminate and pistillate principles of the plant, and the sperm and germ of the animal; that these polar and atomic opposites are lives in production through their reciprocal reactions of an intermediary invisible moral being nature; it is intended that analogously such are the beings that concur in production of the being man.

It is intended that there is the man but in the family of children, infant and adult, about a store of provisions in the hands of the parent,—female, male, or both,—for their safety and subsistence. From the coitions of animals, male and female, there are offsprings, and from those of two-footed and two-handed there are also offsprings, but these are not children ; and the parents and offspring are not man until that offspring shall have been in result of provisions made by its immediate or remote antecedent parents for its support. Between the male and female parents, two-handed and two-footed, as between any other two polar beings, there are reactions in production of offspring,—the disk of nature about that axis of life ; and between such parents and offspring there are reactions in production of the herd or flock,—the disk of nature about that axis of life,—while yet the two-footed and two-handed beings are but animals ; but it is intended that when two such animals, male and female, through their industries, economies and other virtues, shall have accumulated a store of provisions upon which they and their offspring are able to subsist and do subsist in security, such offspring are children, and those parents and offspring, man.

It is intended that the test of whether a being in question be man or animal is in whether the condition to its existence be a previously accumulated store of provisions, moral and physical, for its preservation, safety and support. That of the animal it is distinctive that it endures through successive generations in dependence not upon the provisions that chance to be about it, and of man that no instant of his existence were possible but for reason of some provision, moral or physical, by some previously existing man for its occurrence; and that then only when there comes to be the family of parents and children in existence by virtue of such store which could not have come to exist without is that family man. And it is intended that such store is a nature as the two-footed and two-handed animal is a nature, and the one a nature of life and nature as the other, and that the store is an infinite being finite as is man himself, and that these are to each other as are any other two atomic beings finite in polar relations to each other, and the store life to animal nature, and that the store and animal nature produce man, as electricities reacting produce the spark, or the plant principles the plant, or the animal principles the animal; that in the reaction of these human elements, the store and man, there is the human family —a physiological being as automatic, autonomic, and teleologic as is the individual man himself, or animal, plant, earth, sun, star, or universe; and this in moral consequence of its physical cause, as is man, animal, or plant; and this in its nature to its life, as is man, animal, or plant; and this family under moral ministrations of an invisible genius in linear tradition from God of the universe in force as is the man, animal, or plant.

And it is intended that man, but the family of parents and children about a store of provisions for its support, is analogous to the animal, but the natural group of animated beings about a store of provisions they are instantly accumulating for its support, and that this is in as strict analogy to the plant, but a group of less animated beings about a store of provisions which in their beings possible they are instantly accumulating for its support. That every man, animal, or plant is a being physiological, of kindred beings different of their reciprocal affinities simply in reciprocal limitations of each other, with the difference only that the plant first at this earth's surface, and in representation of dynamic being from the earth and static from the air, is in production of these into a stratum of organic matter,—of the plants possible,—about the earth; and that the animal next in representation of the same dynamic and static beings in the plant is in production of these into a stratum of more advanced organic matter,—of the animals possible—about the earth; and that the man, next in representation of these same dynamic and static beings in the animal, is in production of these into yet more advanced organic matter,—of the man possible,—about the earth; between which, however, there is the further difference that the plant in its beings possible produces from the earth's atmosphere of force the store of organic matter which did not previously exist as such, and the animal in its beings possible but procures from the plant the beings so prepared, and this but as it avails itself of it, and is able to use it in building up itself, while the man to start on the new course of his existence must procure and garner the store of such provisions as are necessary to sustain him in it.

It is intended that these are but the successive stages of the nature of the earth in production of a limiting membrane of vital natures about it, as the plant produces its bark possible, and the animal its skin, and that the plant is endoderm and the animal mesoderm, and man the ectoderm from whom are the architectural projections such as are the capillary appendages of the animal.

And it is intended that,—the plant of nature and the animal of nature,—man is of nature for the reason that he can have come to exist but as he be so produced and continue to exist but as he be so supported, and that he is in exact analogy to the animal and plant.

It is intended that we are possessed, but by deduction from hypothesis, of the start of the agamic family, and but by deduction from the agamic family of the start of the polygamic, but that we have not only hypotheses but phenomena for the start of the monogamic family, and by either find that the family exists but upon previously accumulated provisions for its support in the hands of the male parent for administration; that the monogamic state, whether a constitutional kingdom or a representative republic, is but of such families united about a common store which in theory and fact has been contributed by proprietary male parents, and which in theory is at the disposition but of such parents.

And such the family, it is intended that to each is its tutelary genius ; that in even the agamic family there are the mother and her offspring as natures reacting under the ministrations of an invisible life, which assigns to the mother and her offspring, infant and adult, their reciprocal rights and obligations, in the practice of which there are peoples existing who could not have come to exist or have continued to exist as they do without that nature; but the more is this so with polygamic family, in which reciprocal activities are better organized; and yet the more in the monogamic family, the children of which have the care of both parents, and whose stores of provisions are held by one parent and administered by the other. That families so far as they have been developed are agamic, polygamic and monogamic, and agamic in children about a store in the hands of their unmarried mother, and polygamic in children of several mothers about a store in the hands of their single father, and monogamic in children of a single mother about a store in the hands of their single father; and that of the agamic there are savage stocks, and of the polygamic barbarous tribes, and of the monogamic civil states, under a government by appointment of proprietary male parents, under the protection of a state government theoretically appointed and sustained by the proprietary male parents of the families contributing the public fund for its support.

And such the family of man so far as it is yet evo-involved with capacity for such further evo-involution as may be possible to the best and most of man, it is intended that this man,—consisting in the family,—is in strict analogy to the animal and plant. That the plant is of orders cryptogamic, phanerogamic, endogens and exogens; and the animal of orders radiate, annulate, articulate and vertebrate, and the vertebrate of orders fish, reptile, degitigrade and plantigrade; and man of the orders agamic, polygamic and monogamic accomplished, with a compound monogamic unaccomplished; and that the cryptogamic plant is analogous to the radiate animal and to the agamic man, and the endogenous plant to the articulate animal and polygamic man, and the exogenous plant to the vertebrate animal and monogamic man. And as above the plant there is the animal and above the animal man, that the exogenous plant is analogous to the animal, into evo-involution of which it goes as the vertebrate animal is to the man compounded of unequal races of unilateral man; and that man is analogous to the animal and plant in being but a variation in life to its nature possible. That in either of these families children are born and reared to the opportunity themselves of bearing children who were not without, and that of their associated labors and economies there are more and better provisions made for longer, better and more abundant lives than were possible without association. That in this there are more of animal beings than were possible without, and these coming to exist as human beings there were more human beings than were possible without; and,—intended that there is man but in the family, and that the family of man is analogous to the animal and plant, and that the plant is in evo-involution to its best and most, and the animal also, each a variation, and each the variation in the antecedent animal or plant to its being the more and better sequent animal or plant possible,—it is intended that so by variations, each the evo-involution possible, the man advances to the man possible, and that such is agamic into polygamic man, and such polygamic into monogamic man, and that such will be that of monogamic into compound man; and that man in such variation evolves to its possibilities of being best and most as does the animal or plant, and that the evolution of the family is to its means of subsistence simply as are those of the animal or plant.

It is intended that to its means of subsistence simply are its evo-involutions; that so the alga from infusions of organic matters in the silurean seas become the fungus to procure its food from the soil as it becomes exposed; and so the fungus becomes the lichen to produce it in intermediation of matters from the earth and air; and so the lichen became the moss to the better mediation of such matters; and the moss the equisetum, and this the fern for the same reason, and that thus the cryptogamic and subterranean fern became the phanerogamic aerial and endogenous palm, and thus the palm the exogenous and angiospermous oak; and that thus the sulphosphamonias compound became the amœboid radiate, and this the structured radiate, and this the annulate of successive radiates continuous; and such the articulate from sectional annulates, and the vertebrate from doubled articulates. And so of vertebrates: the fish, originally, also, with the alga, in the silurean seas, became the reptile to its food in marshes forming; and this the quadra-digitigrade to its food from fronds; and this the quadra-plantigrade to its food by capture; and this the four-handed animal to its food by capture, climbing and manipulation; and this the two-footed and two-handed animal to its food from methods of capture, climbing and manipulation.

It is intended that the two-handed and two-footed animal is composite of the two races immediately antecedent. That in its two feet, upon the arches of which from heel to toe it stands, it has the equivalents of the four feet of the plantigrade, and in its two hands of greater flexibility, the equivalents of the four hands of the four-handed animal; and that standing and moving on the four feet of the one, and manipulating with the four hands of the other, it is in condition to co-ordinate the activities of both, and to procure by methods of capture, climbing and manipulation the more of the provisions for subsistence and safety than were possible to either or both its antecedents; but that even then such animal was not man, nor until in the union of two such animals there was a new and compound being of them both, as different from the animal as the animal from the plant.

It is intended that originally in two such two-footed and two-handed animals of opposite sexes there was the superabundance of seed there is in uniaxial animals, and this seed scattered as by such animal in but the reproduction of itself; but that under an inexorable law of its moral being the sexes of this animal were forced to an union in which their reproductive powers were consecrated to each other as fully as are these of the seed of the plant or the ovum of the animal, to the production of the family intermediate of both. That in result of such consecration there is the family, and in this family man; that before the family there was not man, or man before the family; that this variation is from the uniaxial to the biaxial animal. That the simple animal in the continuation of its existence through coition merely is uniaxial, while this as man, in the continuation of his existence through offspring in revolutions on their axis and in orbits of revolution on the axis of parents in coition, is biaxial, and that the animal in living but upon its individual means of subsistence is solitary, while man in living upon associated means is social. That this in man is a variation merely to the means of subsistence; that this in natures antecedent is evo-involution and intended that there is nature in teleologic evo-involution of an universal reality, it is intended that there is man of that nature. And that man is of nature

INTRODUCTION. 83

therefore for the reason that nature, but such reality in evo-involution, is capable of man, but such evo-involution, and capable of man, is cause of man, in that in this universe, but of cause to consequence, capability is cause. And that man is of nature for the reason that he is possible of nature, and possibility consequence—the consequence of nature; and for the reason that if nature, capable, be not cause of man, there is the miracle of cause without consequence; and if man possible be not consequence of nature, there is the miracle of consequence without cause, and that there is not such miracle.

It is intended that man has axioms, reasons, science, knowledge, philosophy, religion and existence even but in acceptance of the truth that there is an universe of cause to an universe of consequence, and an universe of consequence to an universe of cause. That other than this he has not seen and cannot see; that what he has not seen and cannot see is miracle; that to him, therefore, there is no such miracle, and that man is of that nature of which he is the consequence. And that man is of nature but the word of God, or, else, of the anthropomorphic theos of his own imagination. At the verge of nature here, and diffident of duty, man peers into and calls upon the void, and sees but his own image reflected, and hears but the echoes of his own voice; the which he takes for the visage and the voice of his moral monitor invoked, and him for his God, with the concession only that he is also the God of other beings with him in this universe, but concerned in these but as they be tributary to the magnificence of man; and it is intended that this is the idol of the agamic savage and the myth of the polygamic tribe and the theos of the monogamic state, and that this anthropomorphic theos, from whom are the moralities of monogamic man, is of man's own appointment, and to the end but of approving what the man capable of such appointment may wish to do in dominion over other peoples and creatures of this universe.

But it is intended that man is not such self-existent autonomy, and, existing, that he exists but as consequence of some antecedent cause; and that this in the nature of God's univeral word of which he is possible, and that thus he is possible of nature; and that he is in and of the nature of God's universal word for the reason that in this is the only pre-existent being of this universe, and not of cause in this that he is not of cause in any being of this universe, and is therefore such miracle of consequence without cause, he is not.

And it is intended that man is of nature in that nature is the reality in evo-involution, and that the reality is the being finite of the word of God in force; and that man is possible of being finite, and possible of the word of God, and possible of force, and possible of this in evo-involution. And of being finite, for the reason that there is an exclusive universe of being finite into the beings finite of it possible, and that man, not infinite, is being finite, and possible of such universe of being finite. And of the word of God for the further reason that God is the causing cause of all the being of this universe, and this through the word of his own beings infinite in limitations of each other to such cause of the beings of them possible; and that man is possible of the word of God for the reason that he is possible of God, and possible of God for the reason that God, capable of the stars, sun, earth, plant and animal from the universe to man, is capable of man. And of force, for the reason that force is the word of God, and man possible of the word is possible of force; and for the reason that force is infinite being finite, and man possible of this is possible of force, and that force is the only source of space and matter, and that in man there are space and matter possible of that source. And that force is the only source of life and nature, and that in man there are life and nature possible of that source.

And that of nature there is man, for the reason that in man there is nothing not in nature. That in man there are but the matter elements, oxygen, hydrogen, nitrogen, carbon, sulphur and phosphorus, and that there are these in the animal, and these in the plant, saving sulphur and phosphorus, the one but doubled oxygen and the other quadrupled nitrogen. And that in man there are but the physical forces, heat, light, electricity and magnetism; and that there are these in the animal and plant, for the reason that every element of matter in man, animal or plant is but of such forces in reciprocal limitations of each other. And though in man there be the forces, chemical, physical and physiological, there are these in the animal, and all but the psycological in the plant, and that the only force in man not specifically in the animal is the force sociological, which he incurs but as from the solitary animal he becomes social; but that of this force even there are its foreshadows in the hives of bees and hills of ants, and in the herds of brutes and broods of fowls. And that in man there is life; but so also is there in the animal and plant; and nature, but so also is there in the animal or plant; and conscience, so also in the animal and plant.

It is intended that to every being at this earth there is the moral principle of its being physically possible, and that this physical principle is its life, of which its moral being possible is nature; and that this perceptive of conditions incident, is its conscience, to perceive the conditions upon which there is the continuation of its existence; and to order compliance with such conditions, and that this has man, but that this also has the animal or plant, with the difference only that the conscience of the plant is intuitive of conditions experienced in its nature but not recorded in its life, and not therefore recalled for reflection to the exigencies of the current nature of that life. And that the conscience of the animal is naturally intuitive of conditions experienced but not recorded or recalled, but is instinctive of conditions experienced in its life and recorded in its nature but not recalled for reflection to the exigencies of its current life; while the conscience of man is not only intuitive of experiences of life unrecorded and unrecalled as is the conscience of the plant, and instinctive of experience recorded but not recalled as is the conscience of the animal, but is reflective of experienced conditions not only recorded in it but recalled for reflection to the exigencies of the current nature of his life.

It is intended that to each being in nature there is the conscious moral principle necessary to its office in sustaining such nature in existence; that as nature advances to its successive stages from the axis of the universe or earth it advances also in the moral being to sustain it on such stage; that so advanced is the conscience of the plant to prompt the physical, chemical and physiological activities necessary; and such the conscience of the animal to prompt also the psycological activities necessary to its procurement of food and escape of danger; and that such is the conscience of man necessary to the associated methods of procuring food and escaping danger, through which only is there the man possible.

It is intended that every nature, advancing to its higher stages, retains the impressions but loses the consciousness of its experiences in antecedent states while intensely sensitive of its experiences in the state at which it is; and that while man unconsciously is as capable as is the plant of physical, chemical and physiological activities, and as capable as is the animal of the psycological activities upon which his plant and animal natures depend, he is consciously capable but of the sociological activities necessary to his existence in a society of man.

But intended that the conscience of man is but sufficient to sustain him at his time and place in nature; it is intended that so, also, is the conscience of the animal sufficient to sustain it, and so that of the plant, and of the earth and sun, and star and universe, and that for reason of his conscience, therefore, there is not in man that there is not in nature antecedent. And that in man there are axioms in acceptance of the universal law of cause to consequence and consequence to cause upon which man's beings physical and moral depend for their existence. But that so also are these in the animal and plant; that the plant or animal exists but upon the law of cause to consequence and consequence to cause; that, to exist of such law, it must accept such law; that such acceptances are axioms and that unconsciously there are axioms in plants and animals as consciously there are in man.

And that in man there is reason. That between his conscious experiences and their objective causes there are ratios susceptive of comparative observation; that such comparative ratios in sensations to the causes of them there is reason, deductive and inductive, and deductive of consequences unknown from causes known and inductive of cause unknown from consequences known. But this reason with even greater precision has the animal or plant: they are not perplexed by the social engagements of man, but to the extent of their respective offices in preserving their respective existences the plant and animal exercise a reason more faultless than that of man,—more often wrong than right in its suggestions,—and which, at last, is but able to accept the facts which are found to be accomplished.

And that in man there is knowledge; but so also is there in the animal or plant, and that the animal or plant are in the constant practice of truths which it is probable the conscious man will never know, however unconsciously he may himself be in familiar practice of such truths.

And that in man there is religion; but that so also is there in the animal and plant. That religion is the acceptance and practice of the word of God. That to every nature there is in its being merely the mandate that at its place and time it be its most and its best; that it be its most; that obedience to this mandate is religion; that the obedience of the plant or animal is more implicit than is that of man; that he has been misled into theologies by the anthropomorphic theos of his own imagination, which have been as variant from religion as are the rulings of theology from the most and best of men; and, such religion, the animal or plant is more religious than is man.

That in man there is a soul; but that so also is

there in the animal or plant. That this conscience and moral principle in man, through which he takes the precept that he be his most and best to the uses to be made of him, is itself the soul of man; that discharged of its office in the man ceasing to exist, improved or not, it survives him, and, improved, to form into an atmosphere of moral being about man analogously such as is that atmosphere of moral being in which are formed its elements of organic matter about the earth, and these into plants and animals and man; that in this soul of man there are through successive generations successive advancements to that it should be in correspondence, with which there are continued advancements in man to what he should and must be. But, such the soul of man, that analogously such is the soul of the plant or animal; that in each there is the moral principle, to which there is the mandate that it be its best and most; that this advances, and under its moral ministrations in such advancement there is the plant or animal possible.

That to the soul of man there is its heaven; but that so also is there to that of the animal or plant. Intended that there is a moral atmosphere of human being about man analogous to that terrestrial about the earth, it is intended that this is but of the consciences and those the souls of bettered men departed from this life; that not exiled gratuitously to another sphere of being, they are permitted to hover about the race of man, and by their silent ministrations to better and enlarge it; that these are felt in moral suasions and the charities and equities and laws and civilizations of man, which, though quite invisible, are upon him, and, from some such invisible power, with a force which man resists but at the expense of his existence. That this is a heaven, and that there is such heaven for the moral being and plant and animal; that about every class, order, genus, or species of plant or animal there is an invisible moral being to prescribe its course in being possible, and to force it to the adoption of such course; that this can be but of the spirits of antecedent beings, plant or animal; that such assembly of spirits, plant or animal, were a heaven as about every race there is the heaven of the souls of man; and there is a heaven to the souls of man but as there is analogously a heaven to these of animals and plants.

That in man there is property but only as there is property in animals and plants. That of the two-handed and two-footed animals there are hundreds of thousands in man to the one there were without such association; as in the temple there are hundreds of thousands of stones there were not without, and as in the oak there are hundreds of thousands of the beings in the acorn from which it started to become the oak, and as many in the animal of the beings in its ovum; and that as to each stem, or plant, or animal being there has been the cause of its being such as it is, and where it is in such temple, tree, or animal; and that as there is in each the right an l power to retain its existence and position in such temple, tree, or animal, it is intended that this right and power is its property; and that of this property there is an invisible atmosphere of moral being, and this an autonomy of atomic autonomies such as is that about the surface of this earth, the electrical disturbances of which at any one point are felt and may be recorded at another, however distant. That such the atmosphere of properties about the earth, such is that about the temple, tree, or animal; such is that also in man, and about the family and states and state of man. That while the individual man is conscious but of his own individual being and of the means to the preservation of its existence in a horizontal plane of such beings, he is in fact but the unit of an organic group termed the family, itself but the unit of a larger organic group termed the stock, tribe, or states. That each family is about a store of provisions for its support, and each stock, tribe, or state about such store, and the stocks, tribes, and states about such store. That this store is the moral being of the two-footed and two-handed animal developed in the process of its becoming man; that in it, to the extent of his rights, each participates; that this right of participation is his property, and that of these properties there is the moral atmosphere of man integrated and static in visible means to the support and preservation of man, such as are implements, structures and lands appropriated, and dynamic and fluid in tokens of properties we term money; that this is continuous, and in an autonomic atmosphere of power over man apparent in the fact that whoso offers the price,—and by post or telegraph, of property in money becomes its owner. And such the property and supply to the wants of man through which he is integrated into families and states of man, that analogously such is the property of the constituents of the temple, plant, or animal through which they are caused, placed, and sustained in their respective places. And that man does not see himself as such constituent of such being of himself is not more conclusive that such being of himself does not exist than that the blindness of the unit of the temple, plant, or animal to the existence of such is conclusive it does not exist; and that there is property in man but as there be property in plant or animal.

And that man is of nature in that there is no reason that he be not. That nature of the word of God being capable of man there is no reason it be not cause of man. That man being possible of the nature of such word there is no reason that he be not consequence of that word. That God in use of such means to nature will not gratuitously have used other means to man. That there were no necessity for such change of means, and no reason for such change; that there is none in the superior importance of man. That to nature man is less important than the animal of which he is but a specific variation, and the animal of less importance than the plant of which it is but such variation, and the plant of less importance than the earth of which it is but an inconsiderable output and without which the earth to the universe of nature were scarcely less important than it is. Nor can God have wanted man to help him in his work of finishing organic nature at this earth; nor does man intelligently help God in such work when his only effort has been to substitute for God the theos of his own imagination and when his acceptance of the word of God in his own being has been *in invitum* and under protest and but as his being intended has become a fact accomplished; nor does man help God in making the family and state of man, which he refuses to recognize as the work of God, but claims as his own invention and to be discarded when he pleases, and which the firmest monogamic states are now industrious to discard in their discarding the conditions of the family and in putting the property and moral being of the state under proletariate ferments; nor is there reason that God, not seeing fit to use other means to man, shall have allowed other God to use them, or to vest man with other powers than these with which he himself has seen fit to vest him.

Intended that man is of the original endowment of reality in nature or of some additional endowment, it is intended that he is not of additional endowment for the reasons stated; that he exhibits no such endowment; that there is no reason for such endowment and that every instance of such endowment were the miracle of a consequence in man without cause in antecedent nature; which man in his axioms, reason, knowledge, religion and life itself persistently repudiates. And that man is of nature in that there is that in nature of the universe which could not be without man in nature at this earth; that there were not the nature of this universe without, at its time and place,—the nature of this earth, and nor more or less than just this earth; and that there were not this earth as it is but as there be.the plant, or the plant but as there be the animal, or the animal but as there be man, or man but as there be his conscience of conditions incident in making man the man possible. And that man is of nature in that in man there is that which were not without nature. That to the conscience of man, such as it is, there is of necessity man, and to man of necessity the animal, and to the animal the plant, and to the plant the earth, and man were as impossible without such antecedent natures as such natures were without man. And man is of nature if there be man who were so without other source than the word of God through nature, and there is man if there be that which could not be without him, and without which he could not be. That such being is God, or the word of God, or being finite, or force, or the moment of thermal, photal, electric, or magnetic force, or the moment of space, or the molecule, compound or form of matter inorganic or organic, or the plant or animal, or the earth or sun, or star or universe; that as there is not only the one but the every one of these, and that as of these there is man and man of nature, that as there are these or the one of these, there is man of nature. And that man is of nature in that in man there are axioms but in acceptant expressions of a nature of reality; and that in man there is reason but in such expression of such nature; and that in man there is knowledge, religion, and life and space and matter, and man himself but such expression. Nor is it of importance that man repudiates such nature; that he accepts a nature of his own at the hands of the anthropomorphic theos of his own imagination, or that he would prefer a nature of play to a nature of work, or a pleasure garden to a workshop. And that man is of nature in that he exhibits no originating powers; that in being and not of the nature of the word of God it were necessary that he, in some way, originate himself, in which it were necessary that he not only originate his beings but his motives to such beings. But that while obvious that he does not originate his beings as an animal or the beings of that animal, as man it is equally obvious he originates his activities but of motive, and that he does not originate his motive more than does the ball when stricken by the bat. And, such man, that he is at least of nature, whether he be in continuation of nature at this earth or not.

Section VI.

And in Continuation of Nature.

INTENDED thus that of nature there is man, it is intended that man of nature is in continuation of nature; and in continuation of nature in continuing himself in nature, and in giving room and opportunity to animals and plants, and in extending the axis of human nature.

And in continuing himself in nature. Intended that there is an universe of the word of God in force; and that this is life; and that of this in evo-involution there is nature, of which are the stars, sun, earth, plant, and animal from the universe to man,—each in evo-involution of such life and each a nature therefore, and each such sequent nature consequence of antecedent natures, cause,—it is intended that each such sequent nature is in continuation of the course of antecedent natures up to it; and that man is in continuation of the nature of the animal, and the animal of the plant, and the plant of the earth, and the earth of the sun, and the sun of the star, and the star of the universe, and that so man is in continuation of this earth of the nature of the universe, and this, simply, in the continuation of his own existence in nature as such final term of nature at this earth.

And that man is in continuation of nature in giving room and opportunity to animals and plants. Intended that there is a dermal appendage of organic matter to this earth, consisting in plants, animals and man : and the plant as endoderm and the animal as mesoderm ; and man as ectoderm,—it is intended that there is room for the endoderm and mesoderm but as the ectoderm expands ; and that the ectoderm can expand but as there be corresponding expansions of the derms included ; and that so man can enlarge but as he enlarges his means of subsistence and support ; that to this he must have more and better soil, to more and better plants, to more and better animals, to more and better man; that this were giving room and opportunity to animals and plants and,— these natures,—this were giving room and opportunity to natures thus existing more abundantly; and that thus man in continuation of his own nature, simply, is in continuation, through animals and plants, of the nature of the earth and universe.

And that man is in continuation of nature in continuing into the man possible the axis of life in nature from the axis of the universe. Intended that there is an universe of energy in force, and that this is of life and nature, and life cause and nature consequence in evo-involutions, of which there are the stars, suns, and planets, from the universe to this earth ; a planet in evo-involution of which there is its crust of matter, and its atmosphere of force, and its plants and animals and man;—it is intended that there is a continuous and unbroken axis of life and nature in reaction ; that of these in this earth the space centre is life and the crust of matter nature, and of these in the plant the staminate principle is life and the pistillate nature; and of these in the animal the sperm is life and the germ nature; and of these in man the man is life and the woman nature, and the parent life and the family nature; and that thus there is an axis of life and nature through natures possible from the universe to man, and that man in continuation of this axis is in continuation of nature; and in actual continuation of nature to the man possible now existing under the conditions, and in potential continuation of nature to the man possible under possible conditions. And that man is in continuation of the axis of beings static and dynamic in reaction; that there are principles staminate and pistillate,—the one dynamic and the other static, and the one axle and the other disk,—of the plant; and the one sperm and the other germ, and the one dynamic and the other static, and the one axle and the other disk, of the animal; and the one male and the other female, and the one man and the other woman, and the one dynamic and the other static, and the one axle and the other disk, of man ; and these, also, the one parent and the other children in the family of man; and these the one man and the other the state of man in families united to their means of being best and most. And such the axis of a being of beings dynamic and static in reaction that man of this is its ultimate term, and so in its continuation at this earth.

And,—intended that being dynamic is life and being static nature, relatively, and that the axis of these reacting is life and disk nature,—it is intended that man, so far as he yet exists, is in continuation of nature, and that this is the nature of the earth and universe.

It is intended that by induction of the phenomena of the plant apart from other beings at this earth there is the necessary hypothesis of such beings dynamic and static in nature; and by induction of the phenomena of the animal there are such and of man such, and,—this nature,—that there were plant, animal and man successively in continuation of a nature, whether that be of the nature of the earth and universe or not. But by induction of the phenomena of plant, animal and man there is as necessarily the hypothesis of the axis of a being in life and nature from the earth, and through this from the axis of the universe, in the fact that if there be not, the earth, plant, animal and man were each the miracle of consequence without antecedent cause, which man may not consciously accept; and that man, therefore, as far as he has gone, is in continuation of the axis of nature in this earth and universe, and this in the reactions of naturally differentiated man upon the axis of their neutral beings intermediate, the first being that of parents, male and female, in production of children, and the next that of parents and children in the production of the family, and the next that of families differentiated in production of the state. That of these phenomena, the first appears in the human family agamic, consisting in children, infant and adult, about a store of provisions for its support in the hands of its unmarried female parent, and the next in the polygamic family of the children of several mothers, infant and adult, about a store in the hands of a single father; and the next in the monogamic family of the children of a single mother about a store in the single father, each such family differing from the animal or its immediate antecedent but in its capacity for food, —and food life, in its capacity for life, in strict analogy to the cryptogamic, phanerogamic, endogenous and exogenous plant, and to the radiate, annulate, articulate and vertebrate animal, and to the fish, reptile, digitigrade and plantigrade of vertebrate animals; and all,—but the state of man,—analogous to the exogenous plant or the vertebrate animal, which, if possible, has not been yet accomplished; and that man, therefore, to his state of monogamic man, is in continuation of the nature of the earth and universe in his continuation to that extent of the axis of nature from the universe.

And it is intended that he will yet accomplish that fourth stage of man analogous to the fourth in plant and animal, and this in the union of unequal races of man in relations of inequality. That there are unequal races,—in their abilities at least to continue their existences as such; that between races so differentiated as are the agamic and monogamic races there are affinities analogously the same as between the male and female of differentiated man; that of these affinities they are susceptive of coincidence and differentiation on the axis intermediate, as are the male and female of sexually differentiated man; that in the genesis of plant or animal the male is spore and the female nidus; that this also is so in man; that of the sexually differentiated man the male is spore and the female nidus, and of the races of differentiated man the lower is spore to the higher nidus; and that there will be an union of the unequal races of unilateral man in production of compound man, as of the sexes of man there is union in production of the individual man; and that thus there will be an elongation of the axis of human nature as in the fourth order of plants and animals there is of plants and animals, and thus a continuation of nature by man, not only to the present man but to the man possible.

It is intended that there is not now in existence the man possible; that the surface of the earth is capable of supporting thousands to the one man upon it now, and that in man there is the capacity through proper methods of being and activity to produce from the earth's surface the food for such larger population, and the larger population to consume such food, but that there is not the mode of man in existence now capable of that denser and better population possible; that agamic man is not so capable or polygamic man so capable, nor is monogamic man so capable; that to such man it is necessary that there be not only the order, industry, efficiency and economy possible, but that there be duration to the existence to that state of possible man indefinitely greater than that possible to any state of monogamic man. It is useless to argue that any man lower than the monogamic is capable of becoming the man possible, and it is quite demonstrable that monogamic man himself is not; and first for the reason that there is not sufficient duration to the nature of such state. Intended that the nature of advancing man is from the rupture of successive natures, to the nature ultimately possible, as is that of the plant or animal advancing to its possibilities, it is intended that in every state of monogamic man at its maturity there are the pulsations of unsettled life, and these from the proletariate against the proprietary state.

Intended that in every nature there are life and nature, it is intended that these in the monogamic state of man are primarily in the property of the state as life to the state itself,—dependent on that property,—as nature, but secondarily and more obviously in the people of the state as life and the state itself as the nature of that life, and in the theory of such state it is conceded that there is no reason why it might not exist indefinitely.

The monogamic state is of monogamic families, each of the children of a single mother about a store of provisions in the hands of their single father; and the state of such families united is in charge but of that property which proprietary male parents have seen proper, by an instrument termed a constitution, to vest in it for administration to the uses of themselves and families, and there is no more reason why even such unilateral compact should not be respected and endure perpetually. And if there were no change in the relations of such families to each other and the state it would be so respected and would so endure. But a change of relations must necessarily occur. Parents originally proprietary must lose their property from indolence, inefficiency, vice, calamity or crime; and if originally there be provision that upon such occurence they lose their right to participate in the disposition of the common property, that provision will be withdrawn; in sequence of this, adult males not parental or proprietary will acquire the elective franchise, and these males and unpropertied parents will constitute a majority to elect representatives to the legislature, with the power to dispose to their uses of the common property, and with power to draw by taxes indefinitely the property of others to their uses, and to inaugurate, in fact, a game of political poker, at which the players may call upon others to put up the stakes. Upon such conditions the government by imposts will be made to favor the interests of some at the expense of others, and by internal improvements to favor some sections at the expense of others, and there will come to be millionaires to invest in non-taxable securities of the government; taxable property will be without holders; wage-earners will demand more money for less time; all will demand that the state shall educate their children and give employment to those without it, and support the helpless, vicious and criminal classes, and generally, upon even manhood suffrage simply, the government will be made a car of progress upon which all will ride and which none will pull; and, in result of this, property will cease to exist, and the state not able to survive property, there will be an end to that state as certainly as to the individual man whose muscular and nervous tissues are discontinuous from disease or age. But if by possibility in any case this be not so from adult manhood suffrage simply, the deterioration would go on, and first adult women would be allowed to vote, and then children, male and female; and children divorced from parents would start life without employments or capacity of performance, and women, forced to make a living for themselves, would become regardless of their obligation to continue the race of man, and the race of that state of man would stop and the race and state both cease to exist.

It is intended that in every monogamic state, from want of naturally different contracting parties, the constitution, so called, is necessarily an unilateral instrument to mean but that the power to interpret it would have it mean; and as such is not more potent in determining the action of the state than are the resolutions of the sobered man that he will not again get drunk.

But it is intended that in the union of races sufficiently unequal, so that the one has the ability to execute more than it can plan and the other the ability to plan more than it can execute, there is the assurance of its duration in the fact that in such state there can never be the proletariate.

It is intended that every monogamic state is either patriate or proletariate; that at its start it is patriate in its government by appointment of the proprietary male parents of the families involved, which government must act for those appointing it and as such be patriate, but that from the instant of its start it tends to the proletariate.

It is intended that the proletariate is that portion of the population of any state who would not support the state but who would be supported by it; that of this are those who have the elective franchise without the property to be affected by legislation, and that of these are the parents who from misadventure, indolence or vice are without property, and the adult males of families whose properties are yet it in the hands of male parents. That these also are proletariate who would have the government, by imposts or bounties, favor their interests at the expense of others, and those who, whatever their wealth, will not invest in taxable property, and all generally who would rather ride than pull the Juggernaut, including children who would like to be rid of parents and parents who would be rid of children, and women and men who would suppress their sexual propensities or indulge them without contributing to the continuation of their race.

Such the proletariate to which the originally patriate state tends, it is intended that the dissolution is at an early period inevitable; that the tendency is not to make man better but to make him worse; and not to make him continually more abundant in any state, but to extinguish his existence as from such cause has been extinguished the ancient peoples, Nineveh, Babylon, Egypt, Greece and Rome.

And intended that the man possible is the best and most abundant man possible, it is intended that for reason of the proletariate, that man is not possible in the monogamic mode of man; but it is intended that he is possible in a compound mode of unequal races of man united in relations of inequality; that such are the agamic and monogamic races sufficiently differentiated; that such are the agamic negroes and monogamic and Anglo-Saxon whites lately in union in these Southern States; that between races so different there is no miscegenation; that both, however they may severally advance to higher planes of manhood, are relatively, to each other, on parallel planes, and the same as at the start, and as man and woman in union, however they may advance severally through ages of civilization, are in the same relations to each other. Of such state originally patriate there is no transition to the proletariate. The state of two such naturally differentiated beings there is the bilateral being, capable of a bilateral constitution of perpetual duration, and susceptive of instant enforcement, in the injury to individual activity resulting from every instance of its violation. In this there were none to become proletariate, or to ride upon the state, or to misdirect it, or to suspend the reproduction of its population. Early marriages of whites and blacks were possible, and encouraged, as well as the most abundant progeny. And it is intended that in such state there is the possibility of the best and most abundant man; and not only in this, the tendency to such abundant man, but, in the indefinite duration of such state, the time for the maturity of such man; that, in this, man will not only continue the axis of nature as he now does in continuing himself in nature, but will continue that axis to a higher stage of human nature, and so in every sense continue nature.

And intended that there is to be the man possible, it is intended that thus there will be the man possible in continuation of nature, and of a nature of reality throughout the universe; and this the nature of infinite being finite; and this the nature of the word of God in force; and this the nature of a general providence of life in nature to the takers of it possible, and these the stars, suns, planets, moons, meteorites, nebulæ and comets of the celestial sphere; and the forces, matters, plants, animals and man at this earth's surface; and this the nature of a general providence of life in nature to the takers of it possible. That to every such nature there is in its life and nature the mandate that at its time and place it be its best and most, and this simply to man; that at his time and place he can be but the man possible, and can see himself but as the man possible, and can see other natures but as—at their times and places—they be the natures possible; that he has being but of life, and nature and volition but in being, and activity but of volition, and volition but of motive, and motive but of conditions incident, without which the strongest and wisest man were as inert as is the watch unwound; and,—in his utmost capacities from conditions incident,—he is as incapable of seeing or making other natures different from what they are as is the watch of seeing or making other watches different from what they are; and that thus there is not only in fact but to the science of man a nature of reality in life throughout the universe of which man is in continuation at this earth. And this the nature of an universe of force in resolution, and this the nature of God himself in forces of such universe, and this the nature of religion in acceptance and practice by every nature of the word and will of God in force. And that thus man is in continuation of a nature of reality throughout the universe by deduction from the hypothesis of an universe of force the finite word of God; and this that impersonal and transcendent cause and God to man as to other nature of this universe, demanding that he be his most and best and that he submit to the inequalities necessary to that end, as do lives in natures of animal, plant, earth and universe.

www.ingramcontent.com/pod-product-compliance
Lightning Source LLC
Chambersburg PA
CBHW030906170426
43193CB00009BA/754